AF756336

Contents

Acknowledgements

A number of individuals provided invaluable assistance in the preparation of this monograph - in informal discussions and comments on draft material. In particular we wish to acknowledge the assistance of Dr G. Boero (University of Nottingham), Dr E. Hutton (University of Western Ontario), Mr W. McNie (Inland Revenue), Mr A. Olive (H.M. Treasury), Dr J. Martin, Dr D. van der Mensbrugghe, Dr J. Oliveira-Martins and Dr P. Sturm (OECD), Dr. C. Perroni (University of Western Ontario), Professor G. Pyatt and Dr J.I. Round (Warwick University), Mr W. Watts (Department of Environment), Mr A. Webb and Mr R. Weeden (HM Treasury).

Executive Summary

- In September 1992 we were contracted by HM Treasury to prepare a report on applied computable general equilibrium modelling (henceforth CGE). The terms of reference stated that:

  H M Treasury wish to review possible applications of general equilibrium models to various micro-economic (tax, agriculture, trade, environment) areas and to establish:

  i) The value added provided by a general equilibrium model, as compared to possible alternatives

  ii) The main areas where such models are applied with reasonable success, and to identify the under researched areas in terms of UK applications

  iii) The possibilities for using a single general equilibrium model (as a core part of the model) for several of the above purposes, and whether there should be sub-sections of the model showing how particular sections of the economy fit in with/contribute to the overall solution

  iv) The software and informational requirements, and the constraints these place on the form of modelling.

- This monograph is a revised version of the final report on these issues. It evaluates the principles and practice of CGE modelling; assesses its role in policy appraisal, with particular reference to its attributes *vis-à-vis* alternatives; assesses the hardware and software requirements associated with successful modelling; and evaluates the potential for development of this technique in the UK.
- This executive summary reports the findings of the key chapters.

Applied Computable General Equilibrium Modelling: Principles

- One of the most innovative and flexible developments in applied economics in recent decades has been CGE modelling. It is an approach which attempts to simulate numerically the general equilibrium structure of an economy.
- CGE modelling is built upon the Walrasian general equilibrium structure which was developed and refined by *inter alia,* Arrow, Debreu and Hahn. The essential characteristic of a general equilibrium system is that market demand equals supply for all commodities, at a set of relative prices that can be identified.
- In modelling equilibrium systems, one needs to be able to assume that an equilibrium for the economy actually exists. Whilst in theory it is possible to prove

that this is so, in practice it is somewhat more difficult. Any general equilibrium model which aims to capture some level of economic realism, with due allowance for interdependencies, is in general impossible to solve algebraically. The availability of sophisticated algorithms, and the power of modern day computing facilities, means however that such systems can be solved computationally. It is this facility which has been the key technological breakthrough in the development of CGE analysis.

- The first stage in any CGE analysis is setting out the model's structure. The key issues in this process are: dimensionality (i.e. the number of products and factors of production); the functional forms for the key relationships; the level of aggregation; collection of the benchmark data set; and calibration of the model's parameters to that data set. The strategies followed on each of these issues will be determined by the purposes for which the model is to be used, data availability and the software/hardware being deployed.
- Once the structure is in place, the model needs to be solved. A variety of different computer algorithms for solving general equilibrium models are available 'off the shelf', although many applications are customised. Technical change has meant that powerful hardware is readily available. Most CGE applications are now PC rather than mainframe based. Powerful and flexible proprietary software is also readily accessible. As a result, entry barriers to CGE modelling are now relatively low.

Applied General Equilibrium Modelling: Practice

- The burgeoning literature on CGE applications is in part testimony to entry barriers being relatively lower than was the case fifteen, or even ten, years go. However, it is also testimony to the power and flexibility of the approach and its usefulness to policy appraisal. It is a technique that can be applied to a wide range of problems in a wide range of circumstances.
- In reviewing applications, we concentrate on general equilibrium taxation models; trade and integration studies; and the modelling of policy directed at curbing greenhouse gas emissions. This is partly because a great deal of modelling effort has been expended on these issues, partly because the policy focus here is especially sharp. However, we also comment briefly on the wider range of applications.
- Much of the pioneering work in CGE was conducted on taxation models, initially on small-scale purpose-built structures, evolving into larger-scale multipurpose

models aimed at capturing the major distorting effects of complete tax systems. Modelling efforts have embraced both distortion costs associated with particular taxes and subsidies, and the redistributive impact of the tax and subsidy system. The approach has also given insights into the potential impact of the reform of tax structures, including *inter alia*: integration of corporate and personal taxes; replacement of income taxes with progressive consumption taxes; replacement of income tax with a wage tax; and so on.

- A number of themes have emerged from the general equilibrium tax modelling work thus far. One concerns the implications for the equity and efficiency effects of taxes. The conventional wisdom, based on partial equilibrium analysis, that the efficiency costs of the tax system are modest, and that the regime overall does little to redistribute income, has been challenged. General equilibrium analysis points up possibly large welfare costs arising from tax distortions especially at the margin, and a significant redistributive impact. Another important theme which has arisen is the importance of inter-asset tax distortions. The results suggest that the variance in tax treatment across assets may be a more important source of distortion than conventional intertemporal tax distortions.
- Environmental issues have turned out to be an appropriate focus for the application of CGE techniques. In recent years a relatively large number of models have appeared, some country-specific, others multicountry; some are issue-specific, others are used to address a range of issues. Most are directed at assessing the costs of curbing emissions of greenhouse gases. A range of alternative policies has been investigated, including carbon taxes, energy taxes and trade in emission rights. As well as being useful for calculating the costs of alternative abatement strategies, general equilibrium models have also facilitated investigation of the distributional consequences of alternative policies, and the exploration of the interface between environmental and trade policies.
- Compared with tax modelling, environmental models are in their infancy. Nevertheless, a number of themes are already beginning to emerge. First, it does appear to be the case that abatement polices are associated with a real reduction in GDP. Second, there are substantial variations across regions in the magnitude of output loss, and these losses are sensitive to the type of instrument used. In general, the costs of emission controls are higher in developing than in industrialised countries. Third, as theory would predict, the more carefully targeted

the instrument, the lower the costs of abatement policies. In general carbon taxes are more efficient than energy taxes or *ad valorem* taxes.

- The carbon taxes required to secure a given level of abatement vary considerably across models, depending upon how backstop technologies and energy efficiency improvements are dealt with. The 'competition' for CGE in this field appears to come primarily from dynamic optimising models. These probably have a more appropriate structure for dealing with long run consequences, but are less helpful than CGE in evaluating the distributional implications of policy innovations.
- Since the main corpus of trade theory is built upon the two sector general equilibrium model, studies of trade policy and economic integration are well suited to the CGE approach. Moreover, there is a rich agenda of actual and potential policy reforms for analysts to work upon. A large number of studies have been completed. Some are large scale, multisector global models, some are region or country specific, some are sector specific. Among the issues addressed are: the consequences of global multilateral trade negotiations; the impact of deeper regional integration in the EC and North America; the impact of strategic trade policies in particular sectors; the impact of trade policy reforms in particular countries.
- Trade and integration studies are rather more broadly based than either taxation or environmental modelling. Notwithstanding this, the work which has so far been completed has thrown up a number of themes which are notable. First, the output of many recent models with increasing returns and imperfect competition suggests that the gains from trade and integration are likely to be somewhat greater than the orders of magnitude suggested by the calculation of deadweight losses. This arises as a result of the explicit incorporation of pro-competitive effects, and the exploitation of scale economies. Second, there may be a growth bonus from more liberal trade policies, and deeper integration arrangements. Third, as theory predicts, the relative costs of alternative forms of intervention vary consistently.

Evaluation of the Methodology

- The review of applications of CGE modelling highlights a number of strengths but also a number of weaknesses. Having both is not however a shortcoming specific to CGE but a characteristic common to all modelling strategies. As with other techniques strengths need to be exploited, and weaknesses minimised, to make most effective use of the approach.

- Unlike many other approaches to policy appraisal, CGE has solid microfoundations which are generally transparent. Functional forms are explicit and aid the assessment of results, and interdependencies and feedbacks are incorporated. These features mean that CGE is powerful analytically, and make it especially valuable when it comes to assessing the impact of alternative policy interventions.
- The other asset of CGE that makes it distinctive is the facility to probe the distributional consequences of a given policy change. With many methodologies these are neglected, often because it is simply not possible to address them with price endogeneity. Since policy innovation inevitably involves redistribution, this is a key attribute.
- Results from any empirical analysis need to be assessed by reference to the limitations of the model. This also applies to CGE. The limited range of functional forms which are tractable is a constraint, as is the general reliance on calibration rather than estimation. Moreover, unlike more standard econometric analysis, one cannot use statistical techniques to gauge the degree of confidence to place in a particular estimate.
- Other technical limitations relate to the closure rules applied. Typically these involve imposing a balanced budget, or balanced trade, or a savings-investment identity. In the process one may exclude consideration of important relationships.
- Notwithstanding these limitations CGE offers a number of attributes which are unique to the approach and which make the technique an essential ingredient to the process of policy appraisal. To illustrate the value added associated with the approach we contrast it with macroeconometric modelling, time series analysis, fix-price non-CGE models, and partial equilibrium analysis. The first of these is the most relevant. Macroeconometric models are strong in their ability to deal with dynamic accumulation; and also in their ability to encompass monetary variables. Since most are estimated econometrically, it is possible to apply confidence intervals to the assessment of outcomes. All of these attributes are typically lacking in a CGE framework. By contrast however, macroeconometric models are typically deficient on the microeconomic structure of the economy. CGE offers a richer setting for the modelling of the underlying relationships, as well as offering the potential for a full and thorough appraisal of the distributional consequences of a given change. It is clear then that macroeconometric modelling and CGE are complements rather than substitutes.

CGE Modelling and Policy Appraisal

- An important ingredient in the process of policy appraisal is the output of empirical analyses. Applied economics draws upon a rich menu of modelling strategies, including: macroeconometric modelling; panel-based microeconometric modelling; partial equilibrium analysis; input-output techniques, and experimental studies. CGE modelling is a vital ingredient in the portfolio of approaches which can be used to inform policy appraisal.
- It is important to target alternative modelling strategies appropriately in order to maximise the net benefits associated with a particular approach. The suitability of a given strategy will depend upon the objectives and scale of the investigation.
- In general, CGE models are inappropriate for the analysis of small scale, sector specific changes, but are well suited to the investigation of broadly based policy innovations where feedbacks and interdependencies are important, and where the distributional consequences of the change are of interest. The facility to generate insights in these circumstances is an attractive feature of CGE modelling.
- CGE is not well suited to macroeconomic forecasting, but has a role to play in investigating the effects of alternative policy scenarios in the case of economy-wide models, and modelling explicitly the sub-sectors of macroeconometric models in the case of models that are not economy-wide.
- For many large-scale modelling projects, CGE is likely to be the most useful approach given its facility for multi-sectoral modelling - global trade models being a good example.
- The strength of the CGE approach as a key ingredient in a portfolio of modelling approaches is evidenced by the proliferation of models sponsored by international agencies and government bodies - many of which are purpose-built to inform the process of policy appraisal.

Assessment of the Potential for CGE Analysis in the UK

- Little use is presently made of CGE modelling in the UK. In view of the extent to which it has been embraced elsewhere, this is surprising. Both supply and demand factors explain the lack of any serious commitment to the approach.
- Like macroeconometric modelling, CGE analysis benefits from a research cluster strategy. Publicly provided support for model building teams in the UK has been heavily skewed towards macroeconometrics at the expense of other approaches.

- Our enquiries uncovered considerable interest and current activity in CGE modelling across Universities. However, this is presently restricted to individual researchers. With one or two exceptions there is no evidence of actual or latent teams.
- The research agenda for a more serious commitment to CGE modelling certainly exists in the UK, given the obvious interest in taxation issues, integration, environmental issues, agricultural price reform and so on. Moreover given the presently low level of activity in this area, the benefit-cost ratio associated with targeted investment is likely to be high.

Chapter 1. Introduction

The theory of general equilibrium has been a core research area for economic theorists for much of the post war period. The conditions under which a Walrasian market clearing equilibrium will exist, and the characteristics of any such equilibrium are now quite well understood. The notion of a general equilibrium, and the conditions for its existence are more than just a theoretical curiosity: they are central to understanding the properties of a market economy.

The translation of general equilibrium theory into an empirical context has, until comparatively recently, proved elusive. The reasons for this are quite simple - even the most straightforward general equilibrium model is impossible to solve analytically except under extreme simplification (such as a fixed coefficients assumption). We know a great deal about how to derive their *marginal* properties, but that is a long way from finding a solution. Analytically, large scale models which approximate reality are impossible to solve, and the data requirements for estimating such models are just too demanding. Computable general equilibrium (CGE) modelling offers a novel approach to solving the problem of analytical tractability and, getting around (rather than solving), the problem of data constraints.

The basic idea behind a CGE model is simple - one builds an analytically consistent mathematical model of an economy and collects data on those variables for which data are available; then uses the characteristics of the economy at a particular point in time to solve the model numerically. This last stage is performed computationally using powerful computer software. A carefully designed CGE model will have a transparent and theoretically consistent structure, and will offer a vehicle for policy appraisal. The great strength of general equilibrium analysis is that it models the *whole* economy explicitly, albeit under restrictive assumptions. This means that one may consider both problems of the efficiency of resource use, and the equity with which the consequent national income is distributed. There is no other economic methodology that can offer these powers.

CGE models are necessarily an approximation to analytical GE models, in that they operate through numerical solutions which in turn require that specific functional forms be employed, and that the process of calibration is at best suspect. It follows from this that the outcomes of CGE models must often be interpreted as 'insights' rather than absolute truths. The counter-balance is that CGE techniques allow us to examine much more complex issues than those amenable to formal GE analysis, give us some guidance through the maze constructed upon the second best principle, and allow us to consider the consequence of major policy changes (rather than the marginal change analysis traditional to the analytic GE approach).

The availability and accessibility of appropriate software, together with the obvious attractions of general equilibrium modelling, have made CGE a productive research area over the last decade or so. Moreover, it has not only been a core area of activity for academics, its sharp policy focus has led to it being embraced by many governmental and international agencies. The extent of the commitment of the research and policy making communities can be gauged by reference to both the volume of published output, and the range of applications - multilateral trade liberalisation, greenhouse gas abatement policies, economic integration, agricultural support policies and tax incidence - to name but a few.

Thus, CGE has its attractions, as a flexible technique for modelling complicated problems. However, it also has its shortcomings - it relies heavily on secondary data, the reliability of which is often questionable, models are calibrated to a benchmark year which is taken to be an equilibrium, and it offers no formal facility for testing the model structure. But all techniques in applied economics have their strengths and weaknesses. The fundamental issue is whether strengths outweigh weaknesses for the purpose at hand.

In this monograph, we evaluate the principles and practice of CGE modelling, and use this as a basis for reaching a judgement on the value added associated with this particular technique. In Chapter 2 we focus on principles. Here we identify the key theoretical issues in model building, discuss the components of a CGE model and audit the hardware and software requirements of implementation. Chapter 3 reviews applications. Because the range is now so wide we are intentionally selective in targeting tax policy, environmental policy and trade/integration studies. These offer a rich agenda with a sharp policy focus, and are excellent vehicles for illustrating the power, and limitations of this approach. In Chapter 4 we set out in detail the strengths and weaknesses of this approach. In addition we set out what we see as its 'value added' *vis-à-vis* other approaches, in particular macroeconometric modelling. Finally in Chapter 5 we pull all this together in looking specifically at CGE and policy appraisal, exploring in particular whether there is the potential for investment in this approach in the UK. The main text is supplemented by three appendices providing a glossary of CGE terms, the GAMS® coding for a simple CGE model, and a bibliography of the literature.

Chapter 2. Applied General Equilibrium Modelling: Principles

Applied general equilibrium, or computable general equilibrium (CGE) modelling has been a core research area for economists over the last ten years or so. It is an approach to modelling which attempts to simulate numerically the general equilibrium structure of an economy. If successful, the technique allows us not only to represent the general equilibrium structure of the economy, but also to evaluate fully the impact of alternative policy shocks. The theoretical framework which underpins CGE modelling is well known, and well understood. The process of translating the theoretical framework into a numerical model was for a long time frustrated by technology. Two alternative approaches may be distinguished. Johansen (1960) pioneered the use of linear approximations in deriving the counterfactual solution from the initial equilibrium. This approach underpins one of the most ambitious of the CGE models, namely ORANI. Work by Scarf (1969) and Scarf and Hansen (1973), among others, in developing algorithms for numerical solutions provided the foundations for an alternative methodology, in which solutions are derived by solving the full model. This approach underlies much of the recent work on CGE modelling. The proliferation of readily accessible computing power has widened the application of the technique dramatically.

2.1 The Basic Structure of a General Equilibrium Model

Underlying general equilibrium analysis is the Walrasian general equilibrium structure.[1] This was first formalised in the 1950s by Arrow, Debreu and others, resulting in the well-known Arrow-Debreu model, elaborated in Arrow and Hahn (1971).

The Arrow-Debreu model provides the basic analytical framework within which all general equilibrium models may be cast. The model identifies a number of consumers, each of whom is assumed to possess an initial endowment of a number of commodities and factors, and a set of preferences. Utility maximisation leads to demand functions for each commodity and market demands are defined to be the sum of each consumer's individual demand. Commodity market demands depend on all prices, they are continuous, non-negative, homogenous of degree zero (i.e. no money illusion) and must satisfy Walras's Law; that at any set of prices, the total value of consumer expenditure equals consumer income. As regards production, technology is described by either constant or non-increasing returns to scale production functions, and producers maximise profits. The zero homogeneity of demand functions together with the linear homogeneity of profits with respect to prices implies that only relative prices are relevant for these models and absolute price levels have no impact on any equilibrium outcome.

An equilibrium in this model is characterised by a set of prices and levels of production in each industry such that market demand equals supply for all commodities. As producers are assumed to maximise profits, this implies that in the constant returns to scale case no production activity can do better than break even at equilibrium prices.

Many other elements may be built into this simple general equilibrium framework. For instance, the model may be extended to allow for the government sector and an external sector. However, irrespective of the level of additional complexity which is incorporated, the market clearing condition still characterises the equilibrium.

Existence of a general equilibrium

General equilibrium analysis is predicated on the crucial assumption that an equilibrium actually does exist. Proof of the existence of a general equilibrium for the kind of model considered above was first demonstrated by Arrow and Debreu (1954). Extensions to their results have been provided by Debreu (1959) and Arrow and Hahn (1971).

These proofs apply mathematical fixed point theorems to general equilibrium models in order to establish the existence of an equilibrium. The theorems concern continuous mappings of the unit simplex into itself. Supposing that $\boldsymbol{x}$ is an $n \times 1$ vector on the unit simplex, i.e. $\Sigma x_i = 1$, $x_i \geq 0$, then this mapping is such that $\Sigma f_i(\boldsymbol{x}) = 1$, $f_i(\boldsymbol{x}) \geq 0$ where f is a continuous function. Two fixed point theorems are frequently used in general equilibrium theory, those of Brouwer and Kakutani. The first concerns point-to-point mappings of the unit simplex onto itself; the second is concerned with point-to-set mappings. Brouwer's theorem states that if $f(\boldsymbol{x})$ is a continuous function mapping the unit simplex onto itself, then there exists a point z such that $z = f(z)$. Thus z represents a fixed point in this mapping.

We do not pursue the involved theoretical connection between fixed point theorems and the existence of an equilibrium point in a general equilibrium model; we simply note that the applicability of these theorems arises because, in a general equilibrium framework, certain mappings of the excess demand functions, which are themselves a function of prices, can be shown to provide continuous mappings of the unit simplex onto itself, whose fixed points, in turn, meet the conditions required for an equilibrium. Also, the particular value of the price vector for which a fixed point exists in this mapping is simultaneously a price vector for which Walras's law is satisfied. Hence, a fixed point under the mapping corresponds to an equilibrium solution to the model.

Brouwer's theorem is used to demonstrate the existence of an equilibrium in simple pure exchange models. For more complex models, such as those involving production or those which assume additional sectors in the economy (such as a government sector), Kakutani's theorem is generally appealed to in establishing the existence of an equilibrium.

For a particular general equilibrium model some fixed point theorems are relevant only in confirming the logical consistency of that model, in that they demonstrate the existence of an equilibrium point, but do not aid in the computation of the actual equilibrium point itself. This is a separate matter entirely. Thus, non-constructive fixed point theorems provide non-constructive proofs, since whilst they may be used to indicate the existence of an equilibrium they do not, by themselves, provide a means by which the equilibrium point can actually be determined. Others are constructive, in that if a fixed point exists then the algorithm is guaranteed to find it - Scarf's algorithm is a good case in point. Clearly, if a general equilibrium model is to be employed for comparative static policy analysis then actual equilibria must be evaluated.

Computing equilibrium points

For any general equilibrium model which aims to be realistic, the number and functional relationship of the interdependencies and feedbacks among its variables, together with the inherent non-linearity of its functional forms, makes its analytical, or algebraic, solution impossible. This is true even of models with a very simple underlying structure. This means that equilibrium points cannot be determined using standard techniques of algebraic manipulation. Only in very special cases can analytical solutions be derived and the inherent naiveté of these models is such as to render them of negligible practical interest.

In principle, solving a general equilibrium model for its equilibrium point involves no more than finding a correspondence for a set of (non-linear) simultaneous equations, so that any numerical root-finding algorithm, such as the Newton-Raphson algorithm, ought to be applicable to these problems. However, none of these kinds of algorithms is *guaranteed* to work well when solving systems of more than one non-linear equation (multidimensional root-finding being a much more precarious task than optimising a function of many variables). The sheer power of modern day computing facilities has tended to ameliorate this problem to some extent, but up until the early 1970s the lack of such facilities meant that the numerical solution of even relatively small scale general equilibrium models was a largely infeasible task.[2] The initial breakthrough came with the development of Scarf's algorithm (Scarf (1967a, 1967b)) This algorithm was explicitly designed to locate fixed points (equilibrium solutions), and guaranteed convergence. A large number of more efficient and simpler algorithms have since been developed, but they all incorporate the same basic elements as Scarf's original algorithm (hardly any use is made of Scarf's algorithm in modern work).

2.2 Issues in Model Design

Whalley (1991) discusses some of the key issues of model design in the context of large scale models. He identifies these as:

- model structure;
- choice of functional forms;
- choice of parameter values;
- solution methods;
- approaches to evaluating the impact of policy regimes;

- uniqueness of the model's equilibrium.

We shall address each in turn.

Model structure is fashioned first and foremost by the precise purpose of the model. Many models are similar in that they are static; have two factors of production - capital and labour, (with sometimes labour disaggregated by skill); a limited number of goods; inter-industry transactions modelled though input-output fixed coefficient matrices. There are a number of reasons for this similarity. Data availability is an important factor. For instance national accounts typically identify wages and profits (or operating surpluses). This encourages the use of a model with labour and capital inputs. Computational convenience is also important. In the case of the choice of production technologies, for instance, the specification could involve constant, decreasing or increasing returns to scale. Some form of decreasing costs may be appropriate for large ranges of industrial and manufacturing activity. But it has to be recognised that a constant returns assumption tends to make it easier to find an equilibrium concept on which to base the analysis. Finally, it must also be recognised that many of the applied policy issues investigated numerically with CGE models are ones that have previously been examined qualitatively within a theoretical general equilibrium framework. This is particularly true of both public finance and trade theory, where the two sector-two factor model is one that has had a strong influence on applied work.

An important issue in model specification is the treatment of the external sector. The traditional theoretical model is one in which foreign prices, and as a result the terms of trade, are treated as given, and domestically produced, tradable goods are perfect substitutes for foreign goods. The implication of this specification is that changes in foreign prices or changes in the domestic currency price of foreign goods induced by exchange rate or trade policy changes are passed through fully to the prices of competing domestic goods. The realism of this assumption is increasingly questioned, and many CGE models now incorporate the alternative assumption that foreign and competing domestic goods are imperfect substitutes. This is consistent with some empirical evidence that 'pass through' of exchange rate changes to domestic prices is small. It is also consistent with the observed importance of simultaneous importing and exporting of similar goods by the same country. A common way of accommodating this is to use the Armington formulation, which treats similar products produced in different countries as different goods. Use of this formulation has the added advantage of allowing us to characterise sectors in terms of the degree of tradability of the goods they produce.

Some of the other issues in model selection that merit mention are the net savings - capital stock relationship and the treatment of investment. Investment usually is represented as reflecting household and corporate saving decisions, which are based on constant expenditure shares in static models or on inter-temporal utility maximisation in genuine dynamic formations. As a 'quasi-dynamic' approach, static equilibrium models are sometimes sequenced or linked through time to reflect changes in an economy's capital due to net savings: i.e., a series of single period/static equilibria are linked through savings decisions that change the capital stock through time.

Choice of functional form needs to be addressed at an early stage. The choices of utility functions and production functions are fashioned by the need for theoretical consistency and analytical tractability. On the one hand the functions need to satisfy the restrictions required of a general equilibrium model, e.g. market clearing and normal profits in all markets. On the other hand the functions need to generate expenditure and production patterns that can be easily evaluated at any set of prices that are judged as a potential equilibrium set. Convenience, in particular in incorporating key parameters (e.g. income and price elasticities), rather than appropriateness, tends therefore to dominate the choice of functional form. 'Convenient' functional forms, often with strong separability properties, such as the Cobb-Douglas or Constant Elasticity of Substitution (CES), are widely used.

Alongside model selection and choice of functional form, ***choice of the level of aggregation*** has to be confronted at an early stage. Like the other pre-selection issues, this inevitably involves a trade-off between the theoretical attractions of working with more disaggregated data, and the computational complexities of so doing. In practice the choice of aggregation level is determined by what appears to be appropriate to the evaluation of the policy changes under scrutiny, the availability of data, and the availability of appropriate computer hardware and software.

Specifying the benchmark data and ***choice of parameter values*** are the key first steps towards constructing a numerical model. The former involves the construction of a benchmark data set from national income and other major data sources on the technological characteristics of the economy. Typically, data for a single and representative year are employed, but averaging over a period is a possibility. Data are adjusted in order to produce a consistent benchmark data set that is compatible with the equilibrium conditions the model aims to represent. This benchmark data set may be, but is not necessarily a social accounting matrix (SAM).[3]

Parameter values for the selected functional forms are crucial in determining the results of simulation exercises with CGE models. These parameter values are either generated 'exogenously' or through 'calibration' of the numerical model. ***Calibration*** involves fitting the model to the benchmark data set. This may involve some modification of functional forms. However, since no statistical test of model specification is usually involved (a possible exception being the procedure used by Jorgenson), it more typically involves choosing and adjusting the parameters of the model 'endogenously' so that (or until) the model can reproduce what has been taken as the benchmark equilibrium. Herein lies a potential weakness of such a deterministic approach. The assumption of the equilibrium representation by the benchmark data may not be justified, and given that the stochastic elements of economic processes are excluded, confidence in the robustness of policy simulations with the model is thereby reduced. Nevertheless there are strong practical grounds for calibration. Given the dimensions of such models it would be impossible to achieve the same richness in specification via econometric estimation. To estimate simultaneously all model parameters with time series statistical methods would require long runs of data for large numbers of variables. Although partitioning models into blocks of relationships (e.g. into expenditure and production sub-models) is one way of reducing the number of restrictions on identification, and therefore the number of data observations required for estimation, the coverage of time series data may still be inadequate and the partitioning is likely to conflict with some of the general equilibrium restrictions that can be satisfied via calibration.

Not all parameter values are necessarily 'endogenously' determined through calibration however. The benchmark data typically do not identify a unique set of parameter values. In any case with some functional forms it is necessary to pre-specify certain key parameter values. With the widely employed CES functional form, for instance, exogenously determined or pre-specified substitution elasticities are required. Others include income elasticities for consumer goods, elasticities of substitution in production between factors and between (domestic and imported) intermediate inputs, and the elasticity of transformation between domestic and exported goods. This places considerable reliance on careful surveys of the existing literature and on judgement about the studies from which to 'borrow' estimates.

Model solution relies upon an iterative procedure using appropriate algorithms. The basic structure of the model (behavioural equations and functional specification) are combined with the information from the SAM. A solution algorithm is designed to solve for the particular model. The increasing sophistication in computer software means that it is generally data availability rather than solution techniques that constrains this type of applied modelling. But skill on the part of the modeller is required to determine whether the failure of the model to converge towards the benchmark equilibrium is a product of the solution method or of the functional forms and specific parameter values adopted. Where it is the latter some re-calibration may be required in order to produce convergence towards a final numerical solution.

CGE models are of interest primarily because of the opportunities they offer in ***evaluating the impact of policy changes***. By specifying new values for each policy instrument separately, or for a range of instruments simultaneously, it is possible to solve the model to identify a new counter-factual equilibrium. It is possible therefore to evaluate alternative reform packages or to compare specific reforms of alternative magnitudes by comparing the counter-factual and benchmark equilibria. Comparison of alternative equilibria means that the policy appraisal is medium to long term in nature. In addition to counterfactual policy analysis, the models can also be used to investigate other counterfactuals, for example changes in endowments or changes in preferences. Figure 2.1 summarises the various steps involved.[4]

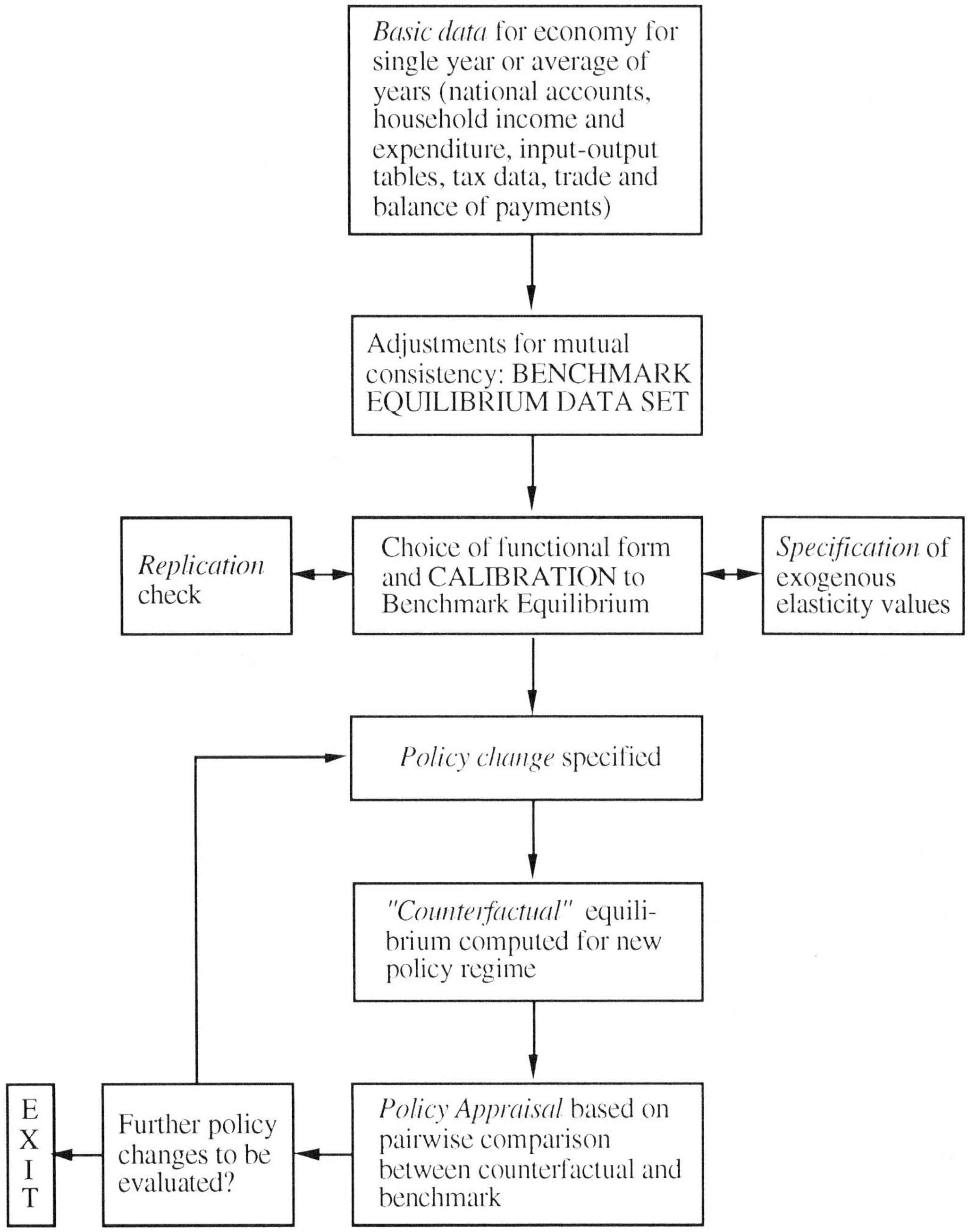

Figure 2.1: Calibration procedures and model use in a typical CGE model

In order to make normative assessments of policy it is necessary to measure economic welfare. The most commonly used measures are the Hicksian compensating (CV) or equivalent variations (EV); the former starts from the new equilibrium and asks how much income needs to be added to subtracted to return consumers to their original utility level; the latter starts from the original equilibrium and measures the change in income required to reach the new utility level. (For a welfare-raising change CV is negative and EV is positive.) Where the model provides detailed information on CVs or EVs (i.e. gainers and losers in utility terms), then the policy analyst may be interested in distributional effects, and it may not be necessary to aggregate individual welfare effects. Where net evaluations are required it is usual to aggregate CVs (or EVs) across households. There are obvious theoretical difficulties in interpreting the resulting net measure as an indicator of social welfare.

Of course problems of distribution and aggregation are often abstracted from in applied trade models by assuming only one representative household or consumer. In this case the aggregate efficiency and welfare effects of trade policy change are directly observable. However, the potential for evaluating distributional consequences exists, and many see this as one of the great strengths of CGE modelling.

2.3 A Simple Numerical Example of an Applied General Equilibrium Model

A numerical example is a convenient means of illustrating the basic steps involved in applied general equilibrium analysis. We consider here the simple tax model of Shoven and Whalley (1984).

Model specification and functional forms

In this example there are two final goods (manufacturing and non-manufacturing), two factors of production (capital and labour) and two classes of consumer (a 'rich' group which owns all the capital and a 'poor' group which supplies all the labour). There are no consumer demands for factors (i.e. no labour-leisure choice).

Each class of consumer generates demand by maximising a CES (constant elasticity of substitution) utility function, subject to its budget constraint. The CES utility function is given by

$$U_c = \left(\sum_{i=1}^{2} \left(a_{ic} X_{ic} \right)^{(\gamma_c - 1)/\gamma_c} \right)^{\gamma_c/(\gamma_c - 1)} \qquad \text{where } \sum_{i=1}^{2} a_{ic} = 1$$

where X_{ic} is the quantity of good i demanded by consumer c, the a_{ic} are share parameters and γ_c is the elasticity of substitution in consumer c's CES utility function. Consumer c's budget constraint is

$$P_1 X_{1c} + P_2 X_{2c} = I_c$$

where I_c is the income of consumer c, defined as

$$I_c = P_L W_{Lc} + P_K W_{Kc}$$

where P_1 and P_2 are the prices the consumer faces for the two goods, W_{Lc} and W_{Kc} are consumer c's endowments of labour and capital, P_L and P_K are the price of labour and capital. Maximising U_c subject to the budget constraint yields the demand functions

$$X_{ic} = a_{ic}^{\gamma_c} I_c \Big/ \left(P_i^{\gamma_c} \sum_{j=1}^{2} a_{jc}^{\gamma_c} P_j^{(1-\gamma_c)} \right)$$

for i = 1, 2 and c = 1, 2. In what follows we will suppose that c = 1 represents the 'rich' consumer group, c = 2 represents the 'poor' consumer group. Also we assume that i =1 refers to manufactured goods and i = 2 to non-manufactured goods.

The production functions are also assumed to be CES. These functions are given by

$$X_i = \phi_i \left(\delta_i L_i^{(\sigma_i - 1)/\sigma_i} + (1 - \delta_i) K_i^{(\sigma_i - 1)/\sigma_i} \right)^{\sigma_i/(\sigma_i - 1)}$$

for i = 1, 2. Here Q_i denotes the output of industry i, ϕ_i is a scale (or units) parameter, δ_i is a distribution parameter, K_i and L_i are capital and labour inputs and σ_i is the elasticity of factor substitution. From this production function, and the assumption of cost minimisation, the following expressions for factor demands, as functions of factor payments, can be derived

$$L_i = (1/\phi_i) Q_i \left(\delta_i + (1 - \delta_i) \left(\delta_i P_K / ((1 - \delta_i) P_L) \right)^{(1-\sigma_i)} \right)^{\sigma_i/(1-\sigma_i)}$$

$$K_i = (1/\phi_i)Q_i\left((1-\delta_i)+\delta_i\left((1-\delta_i)P_L/(\delta_i P_K)\right)^{(1-\sigma_i)}\right)^{\sigma_i/(1-\sigma_i)}$$

In this example there are therefore six utility function parameters (a_{ic} and γ_c for i = 1, 2 and c = 1, 2), six production function parameters (ϕ_i, δ_i and σ_i for i = 1, 2) and four exogenous variables (W_{Lc} and W_{Kc} for c = 1, 2).

The very simple structure of the above model does not incorporate any policy parameters, so we cannot subsequently solve for a counterfactual equilibrium under different assumed values of policy parameters. However, it is fairly straightforward to augment the basic model to allow, for instance, the imposition of *ad valorem* taxes on factors. In the example used by Shoven and Whalley, government sector involvement is simplified to the extent that tax revenues are used solely for disbursements back into the economy. This creates the condition that tax revenues generated must equal government transfers collected by the public. Thus two extra parameters are required to model the government sector: a tax rate and the share of total tax revenues disbursed to each consumer group. Defining the tax rate on capital (labour) in sector i as t_{Ki} (t_{Li}), the share of tax revenues disbursed to consumer group c as t_c ($t_1 + t_2 = 1$), and total tax revenue as T, the factor demand equations are modified to

$$L_i = (1/\phi_i)Q_i\left(\delta_i+(1-\delta_i)\left(\delta_i(1+t_{Ki})P_K/((1-\delta_i)(1+t_{Li})P_L)\right)^{(1-\sigma_i)}\right)^{\sigma_i/(1-\sigma_i)}$$

$$K_i = (1/\phi_i)Q_i\left((1-\delta_i)+\delta_i\left((1-\delta_i)(1+t_{Li})P_L/(\delta_i(1+t_{Ki})P_K)\right)^{(1-\sigma_i)}\right)^{\sigma_i/(1-\sigma_i)}$$

and the income equation is now given by

$$I_c = P_L W_{Lc} + P_K W_{Kc} + t_c T$$

An equilibrium solution for this model is given by the four price variables P_1, P_2, P_L and P_K, together with the tax revenue T that meet the equilibrium condition that market demand equals market supply for all inputs and outputs, that the zero profit condition applies in both industries, and that the government budget equation balances (transfers equal total tax revenues). In algebraic terms, we require the solution of the following system of equations:[5]

Labour demand equals supply

$$L_1 + L_2 = W_{L1} + W_{L2}$$

Capital demand equals supply

$$K_1 + K_2 = W_{K1} + W_{K2}$$

Demand for manufactured goods equals supply

$$X_{11} + X_{12} = Q_1$$

Demand for non-manufactured goods equals supply

$$X_{21} + X_{22} = Q_2$$

Zero profits in manufactured goods industry

$$P_1Q_1 = (1 + t_{L1})P_LL_1 + (1 + t_{K1})P_KK_1$$

Zero profits in non-manufactured goods industry

$$P_2Q_2 = (1 + t_{L2})P_LL_2 + (1 + t_{K2})P_KK_2$$

Balanced government budget

$$t_1T + t_2T = t_{L1}P_LL_1 + t_{K1}P_KK_1 + t_{L2}P_LL_2 + t_{K2}P_KK_2$$

The benchmark data set

Shoven and Whalley (1984) provide benchmark data for all the quantity variables in the model. As is standard, these data are given in value terms, which means that units need to be chosen for goods and factors such that unique price and quantity observations can be obtained. Since we are only concerned with changes in the values of relative prices between benchmark and counterfactual equilibria, a commonly used units convention, originally adopted by Harberger (1959, 1962), is to choose units for both goods and factors so that they all have a price of unity in the benchmark equilibrium. The Shoven and Whalley data are summarised in Table 2.1.

TABLE 2.1: THE SHOVEN AND WHALLEY BENCHMARK DATA

PRODUCERS		
	Manufactures (i = 1)	Non-manufactures (i = 2)
Consumer Demands§		
Rich consumers (c= 1)	X_{11} = 16.110	X_{21} = 18.227
Poor consumers(c= 2)	X_{12} = 18.782	X_{22} = 41.212
Total demands	$X_{11} + X_{12}$ = 34.892†	$X_{21} + X_{22}$ = 59.439
Product Supplies§		
	Q_1 = 34.898†	Q_2 = 59.439
Input demands		
Labour	L_1 = 26.366	L_2 = 33.634
Capital	K_1 = 8.532	K_2 = 25.805
Cost of inputs	$L_1 + K_1$ = 34.898	$L_2 + K_2$ = 59.439
Production Parameters		
Elasticity of substitution¥	σ_1 = 2.0	σ_2 = 0.5
CONSUMERS		
	Rich consumers (c= 1)	Poor consumers(c= 2)
Consumer Demands		
Manufactures (i = 1)	X_{11} = 16.110	X_{12} = 18.782
Non-manufactures (i = 2)	X_{21} = 18.227	X_{22} = 41.212
Total demands	$X_{11} + X_{21}$ = 34.337	$X_{12} + X_{22}$ = 59.994†
Factor incomes		
Labour	W_{L1} = 0.000	W_{L2} = 60.000†
Capital	W_{K1} = 34.337	W_{K2} = 0.000
Total factor incomes	$W_{L1} + W_{K1}$ = 34.337	$W_{L2} + W_{K2}$ = 60.000
Demand Parameters		
Elasticity of substitution¥	γ_1 = 1.5	γ_2 = 0.8

§ quantities and values since all prices = 1

† the discrepancies are a consequence of the numerical solution

¥ assumed values

Calibration to the benchmark data set

Given the benchmark data, the only unknown variables in the system are the parameter values a_{ic}, ϕ_i and δ_i and these can be determined through calibration to the benchmark data, assuming that these data represent an equilibrium of the model. Shoven and Whalley also assume that all factor tax rates t_{Ki} and t_{Li} are set equal to zero in the benchmark equilibrium so that the model collapses to a simpler non-tax model with $T = 0$ and the parameters t_c redundant. For this simple model, the first order conditions for cost-minimisation allow us to determine the distribution parameters, δ_i, of the production functions. We can obtain values for the demand share parameters, a_{ic}, in a similar fashion. The scale parameters in production, ϕ_i, can be determined from the zero profit condition for equilibrium.[6] Their values in the benchmark equilibrium solution are given in Table 2.2.

TABLE 2.2: DERIVED PARAMETER VALUES

	Manufactures	Non-manufactures
Demand share parameters		
Rich consumers	$a_{11} = 0.469$	$a_{21} = 0.531$
Poor consumers	$a_{12} = 0.313$	$a_{22} = 0.687$
Production scale parameters	$\phi_1 = 1.860$	$\phi_2 = 1.966$
Production distribution parameters	$\delta_1 = 0.637$	$\delta_2 = 0.629$

Counterfactual analysis

As a simple example of a counterfactual equilibrium solution, Shoven and Whalley examine the effects associated with imposing a 50% tax on capital in the manufacturing sector; thus $t_{K1} = 0.5$. All other factor tax rates are assumed to remain at zero. The share of tax revenues disbursed to the 'rich' consumer group is 40%, so that $t_1 = 0.4$ and 60% is disbursed to the 'poor' consumer group, hence $t_2 = 0.6$. The wage rate P_L is arbitrarily set equal to unity as a numéraire, so that all other goods and factors are priced relative to labour. As all parameter values are now known (either given as basic data or evaluated through calibration), the unknown variables of the system to be determined from the counterfactual equilibrium are the price variables P_1, P_2, and P_K, the quantity variables X_{11}, X_{21}, K_1, L_1, and the tax yield T. The variables X_{12}, X_{22}, K_2 and L_2 may then be determined directly from the model. The values of these variables are given in Table 2.3.

TABLE 2.3: THE COUNTERFACTUAL SOLUTION

GOODS MARKETS		
	Manufacturing (i = 1)	Non-manufacturing (i = 2)
Prices	$P_1 = 1.048$	$P_2 = 0.920$
Sales /Purchases		
Rich consumers (c = 1)	$X_{11} = 12.577$	$X_{21} = 17.302$
Poor consumers (c = 2)	$X_{12} = 18.741$	$X_{22} = 45.343$
FACTOR MARKETS		
	Labour	Capital
Prices	$P_L = 1.000$	$P_K = 0.821$
Sales/Purchases		
Manufacturing	$L_1 = 25.997$	$K_1 = 5.546$
Non-manufacturing	$L_2 = 34.003$	$K_2 = 28.791$
GOVERNMENT		
Tax revenue	$T = 2.277$	

The values of other variables may then be derived from these using the model specification; these derived values are given in Table 2.4.

When compared to the benchmark equilibrium, we see that the net-of-tax cost of capital has fallen; however, the increase in the tax-inclusive cost of capital has led to less capital-intensive manufacturing production. Less manufacturing production and more non-manufacturing production now takes place. A simple calculation of group incomes shows that the total expenditure of 'poor' (labour-owning) consumers has risen, whilst that of 'rich' (capital-owning) consumers has fallen.

TABLE 2.4: DERIVED VARIABLES IN THE COUNTERFACTUAL EXAMPLE

PRODUCERS		
	Manufacturing ($i = 1$)	Non-manufacturing ($i = 2$)
Total sales	31.318	62.644
Sales values	32.821	57.633
Factor costs (exc. taxes)		
Labour	25.997	34.003
Capital	4.553	23.637
Tax payments		
Labour	0.000	0.000
Capital	2.277	0.000
Factor costs (inc. taxes)		
Labour	25.997	34.003
Capital	6.830	23.637
Totals	32.827	57.640
FACTOR MARKETS		
	Labour	Capital
Payments/receipts		
Rich consumers	0.000	28.191
Poor consumers	60.000	0.000
Government	0.000	2.277
Total	60.000	30.467
CONSUMERS		
	Rich consumers ($c = 1$)	Poor consumers ($c = 2$)
Incomes		
Sales of labour	0.000	60.000
Sales of capital	28.191	0.000
Transfer from govt	0.911	1.366
Totals	29.101	61.366
Expenditures		
Manufactures	13.181	19.641
Non-manufactures	15.918	41.716
Totals	29.099	61.356

TABLE 2.4: continued

GOVERNMENT		
	Receipts	Payments
Tax revenue	2.277	
Paid to rich consumers		0.911
Paid to poor consumers		1.366
Totals	2.277	2.277

A simple measure of the welfare change between the benchmark and counterfactual equilibria can obtained by calculating the Hicksian equivalent variation (HEV) for each group, and in aggregate.

$HEV_1 = -4.552$

$HEV_2 = 4.003$

$HEV_1 + HEV_2 = -0.549$

By this criterion, the redistribution caused by the relative factor price change has meant that the welfare of 'poor' consumers rises and that of 'rich' consumers falls. That there is an aggregate welfare loss reflects the fact that the tax is distortionary. The complete GAMS code for this simple example is given in Appendix C.

2.4 Computational Issues in Applied General Equilibrium Modelling

Having outlined the basic theoretical structure of a CGE model, evaluated the key issues in model design, and worked through a specific case, we now turn to computational issues. This section outlines some of the computational considerations that are relevant to building and using applied general equilibrium models. It is augmented by Appendix B, which discusses hardware and software requirements.

Algorithms for Solving General Equilibrium Models

At present there are a variety of algorithms available for solving general equilibrium models. The first algorithm explicitly tailored to finding fixed points, or equilibrium solutions, was developed by Herbert Scarf (Scarf (1967a, 1967b)). The elegance of this algorithm lies in the fact that it is based on the proof of existence of an equilibrium and actually follows the steps used in that proof. Further, it is guaranteed to work without any constraints on the specification of the model (apart from that of Walras's Law being satisfied). Scarf's algorithm also guarantees convergence to an approximate fixed point, or equilibrium solution, within a finite number of steps (the so-called 'no cycling' property introduced by Lemke and Howson (1964)). Although Scarf's original algorithm was quite inefficient from a computational viewpoint, subsequent modifications have greatly increased its efficiency and applicability whilst retaining the same basic properties of Scarf's algorithm, in particular its guaranteed convergence properties. These developments include Merrill's algorithm (Merrill (1972)), the algorithm of Van der Laan and Talman (Van der Laan and Talman (1979)), and Rutherford's MPS.GE , which uses the linear complementarity methods of Mathiesen.

Alternatively, Newton-type algorithms are often used to solve general equilibrium models. These well-known methods solve the model equations by making a succession of linear approximations to the underlying non-linear model and seek simultaneous zero points for the equilibrium solution. As such, these methods are less specific to general equilibrium models in that the fixed point nature of the equilibrium solution is not explicitly incorporated. Also, Newton-type methods do not guarantee convergence, and this tends to lessen their appeal to many mathematical economists, who prefer the elegance of the Scarf-type algorithms. Although these methods lack the specificity and consequent efficiency of the Scarf-type methods, the sheer speed of modern computers has done much to minimise these disadvantages. As with Scarf-type methods, Newton-type algorithms also allow great flexibility in model specification (because excess demand functions are smooth) and have been extensively used in the area of applied general equilibrium modelling.

Hence, something of a divide currently exists between the theory and application of computational general equilibrium techniques. In the theoretical work, attention is focused primarily on computational procedures that are known to converge. In applications, however, guaranteed convergence is often sacrificed in favour of computational procedures that require less execution time.

Since both types of solution method mentioned above impose very few constraints on model development for 'smooth' problems, the choice between the two effectively becomes a question of the relative efficiency of the algorithms. Unfortunately, this is not a straightforward matter. A particular algorithm may perform efficiently with certain functional forms and more poorly with others. For instance, Newton-type methods work well with near-linear models but become much less efficient as the degree of non-linearity of the model increases. Alternatively, an algorithm may be very efficient if the dimensions of the general equilibrium problem are small, but relatively slow with larger scale problems. In broad terms, any algorithm will solve a standard model, but some of the more sophisticated general equilibrium models can only be solved by a certain kind of algorithm. It is therefore important that the applied modeller has experience of using a variety of algorithms and is aware of their different properties in different models.

The methods of computation of counterfactual equilibria discussed above involve solving the entire system of non-linear equations which comprise the model each time a policy change (change in a parameter value) is specified. As such, the computational burden involved in finding a counterfactual equilibrium is of the same order of magnitude as is involved in calibration to the benchmark equilibrium solution. An alternative approach pioneered by Johansen (1960) replaces the system of non-linear equations with a linear approximation which allows counterfactual equilibria or, more specifically, the difference between benchmark and counterfactual equilibrium solutions, to be computed from simple linear matrix operations. This approach is appropriate to situations where there are only marginal differences between the benchmark and the counterfactual equilibria; however, non-marginal changes, may be approximated by a succession of marginal changes. Although this approach still requires that the non-linear system is solved to obtain a benchmark equilibrium in the usual way, subsequent counterfactual analysis does not require that the model has to be re-solved. Thus, the potential for computational saving is considerable.

2.5. Summary and Conclusions

- General equilibrium models build upon the general equilibrium structure associated with Walrasian market clearing at an identifiable set of prices.
- A number of proofs have been developed which establish the existence of an equilibrium, utilising mathematical fixed point theorems.
- Given the complexity of any general equilibrium model which aims to capture some degree of realism, algebraic solutions are impossible. The essence of CGE is the deployment of numerical algorithms to solve such models.
- Model structures are driven first and foremost by the precise purpose of the model - this will fashion issues like dimensionality, openness, intertemporal linkages etc..
- Choice of the level of aggregation involves a trade-off between the theoretical attractions of working with highly disaggregated data, and the computational complexities of so doing. Once the level of aggregation is set, and the benchmark data set compiled, the model can be calibrated.
- The process of calibration involves choosing and adjusting the parameters of the model endogenously, until it can reproduce the benchmark equilibrium. The process has the advantage of being deterministic, but unlike econometric modelling we are unable to apply diagnostic tests which give some indication of the confidence we can place in a particular set of results.
- CGE can be used for policy appraisal by either specifying new values for each policy instrument separately, or by solving the model for a new counter factual equilibrium. The welfare consequences of alternative scenarios are typically assessed by reference to Hicksian compensating or equivalent variations.
- There are now a variety of algorithms available for solving general equilibrium models, some of which allow great flexibility in model specification.
- Hardware requirements are determined by model complexity - small scale models can be handled by standard PC technology, large multi-country, multi-product models may require mainframe support.
- Software may be off the shelf or purpose built. The latter may use GAUSS or MATHEMATICA, the former will typically use GAMS, MPS/GE or GEMPACK.[7] Model building software is now relatively accessible, and comparatively user friendly, with many functional forms 'hard-wired' into the programme.

Chapter 3. Applied General Equilibrium Modelling: Practice

The growing sophistication of software, the availability of hardware, and growing interest in applied general equilibrium modelling have resulted in a proliferation of applications. The bibliography in Appendix D provides an indication of just how extensive the range of applications now is, and the rich diversity of country specific/regional/global applications. The areas where the approach is now routinely applied include the modelling of:

- tax incidence and tax reform
- global trade flows and trade liberalisation
- economic integration
- economic effects of curbing greenhouse gas emissions
- policy reforms in developing countries
- price reforms in agricultural markets
- imperfect competition and market behaviour

The range of applications is simply too wide, and the literature too deep to countenance a comprehensive survey in a monograph of this nature. Instead we concentrate our attention on three areas of application - general equilibrium tax models; trade and integration studies; carbon tax studies. These are areas where major modelling efforts have been underway for sometime, and where the policy focus is particularly sharp. In each case we review the literature and assess what we can learn from it.

3.1 General Equilibrium Tax Models[8]

In the early 1970s, Shoven and Whalley (1973) showed how a variety of taxes can be simultaneously incorporated into a basic general equilibrium approach. These include income taxes, modelled as taxes on personal incomes at progressive rates; corporate taxes, modelled as taxes on inputs of capital by industry; property taxes, also modelled as taxes on factor inputs; social security taxes, modelled as payroll taxes; and sales and excise taxes, modelled as either output taxes by industry or consumption taxes by households.

They demonstrated how it is possible to move beyond small-dimensional illustrative examples and build computational general equilibrium models representative of actual economies. An early example was Whalley's (1973) general equilibrium model of the United Kingdom, designed to analyse the effects of several tax changes occurring at the time of British entry into the European Economic Community.

To understand the general equilibrium approach to tax policy modelling, it may help to delve more deeply into individual models to see how they have been constructed, what issues have been analysed, and what the main findings have been. Here, we follow Whalley (1989) in summarising seven tax based modelling efforts, reflecting a variety of approaches. Two are larger-scale, multipurpose models which aim to capture the major distorting effects of complete tax systems. Two are smaller-scale, more issue-specific modelling efforts focused respectively on tax issues associated with risk-taking and intertemporal allocation. The final three show the evolution of models into newer areas. Tables 3.1 and 3.2, reproduced from Whalley (1989), summarise the main features and policy implications of results for each of these.

Overview of the key models

The large multipurpose models were the first models developed, typically in the mid 1970s to early 1980s, with the aim of allowing for simultaneous analysis of several tax changes, usually as part of a package or a tax reform. An early example is Piggott and Whalley (1985b), who developed a large-scale model in the mid-1970s to evaluate the distorting effects of the tax and subsidy system in operation in the United Kingdom at the time. This model was calibrated to a 1973 data set, a year in which major changes were made in the U.K. tax system, including the introduction of VAT.

TABLE 3.1 MAIN CHARACTERISTICS OF ELEVEN TAX POLICY MODELS

Model	*Economy Studied*	*Base year for data*	*General-purpose or issue-specific*	*Dimensionality*	*Taxes covered*	*Function forms*
Piggott and Whalley	UK	1973	General-purpose	33 industries, 100 household groups	All major taxes and subsidies	Nested CES-LES
Ballard *et al.*	USA	1973	General-purpose	19 industries, 15 consumer goods, 12 household classes	All major federal, state and local taxes	Nested CES-fixed coefficient (production); nested CES-Cobb-Douglas (consumption)
Slemrod	USA	1977	Issue-specific: capital income	9 income classes, 4 goods, 6 assets	Personal and corporate income taxes, property taxes	Cobb-Douglas (consumption)
Summers	USA	No historical data used (rough approxima-tion)	Issue-specific: capital taxation	1 good, 1 household sector	Capital taxes	Constant elasticity with constant rate of discount (utility)
Goulder and Summers	USA	1973	Issue-specific: asset prices and investment	5 industries, 15 consumer goods, 1 household	Major federal, state and local taxes	CES-fixed factor (production); fixed expenditure shares (consumption)
Galper, Lucke and Toder	USA	1983	Issue-specific: capital stock allocation	3 suppliers of capital 400 representative households, 5 assets	Statutory corporate tax, entire schedule of personal taxes	Unit-elastic demand for capital
Jorgenson and Yun	USA	1955-80 (econome-tric estima-tion)	Issue-specific, efficiency effects of taxes on capital allocation	1 consumer, 3 sectors, 4 commodity groups	Sales tax on consumer and investment goods, income tax on capital and labour services, property taxes	Intertemporal logarithmic utility function; translog price functions with two-stage allocation process (production)
Piggott	Australia	1972-73	General-purpose	12 household groups, 18 domestic and 14 foreign industries	All major taxes and subsidies	nested CES (demand); CES value-added (production)
Keller	Netherlands	1973	General-purpose	4 demand sectors, 4 industries	Taxes on consumer goods and services, on capital goods, imports, labour capital and corporate income; lump sum taxes	Nested-CES (demand and production)
Kehoe and Serra-Puche	Mexico	1977	General-purpose	35 goods (including 14 production goods), 12 consumer groups	All major taxes including sector-specific taxes	Fixed coefficient Cobb-Douglas (production); Cobb-Douglas (demand)
Kehoe *et al.*	Spain	1980	General purpose	12 production sectors, 27 goods, 8 households, 2 foreign sectors	Major taxes including turnover tax on production, social security taxes, taxes on foreign trade	Cobb-Douglas (demand and production)

Source: Whalley (1989)

The model is static. Model production functions allow for substitution between factors according to CES value-added functions. Joint production and intermediate use of goods in production are incorporated using a fixed-coefficient structure. Literature sources are used to select a central set of production and demand function elasticity values, around which sensitivity analysis is conducted.

TABLE 3.2 POLICY IMPLICATIONS OF RESULTS FROM 11 TAX POLICY MODELS

Model	*Policy Implications*
Piggott and Whalley	Distortionary effects of tax-subsidy system higher than conventionally assumed (6-9 percent of NDP); major sources of welfare loss are housing subsidies, excise taxes, capital income taxes.
Ballard *et al.*	Integration of corporate and personal taxes yields significant welfare gains; introduction of progressive consumption tax yields similar gains; both policies can be Pareto-improving for income classes modelled.
Slemrod	Indexing of tax system leads to efficiency gains; lowest income classes slightly worse off, highest income classes substantially better off.
Summers	Increase in output and welfare from shift from capital taxation to consumption taxation much large than previously though: increase in welfare for representative consumer equivalent to approximately six years' income.
Goulder and Summers	Reduction of corporate income tax from 46 to 34 percent raises firm values significantly in all industries modelled (15 to 21 percent); reduction of investment tax credit reduces capital stock and productivity of capital; a combination of these policies reduces aggregate capital stock over the longer term.
Galper, Lucke and Toder	Introduction of flat tax rates and integration of corporate and personal taxes each lead to expansion of corporate sector in the absence of portfolio effects; inclusion of portfolio effects weakens and in some cases reverses this results
Jorgenson and Yun	Tax reform of 1981-82 increased potential economic welfare by 3.5 to 4 percent of 1980 private national wealth; neutralising treatment of assets between corporate and noncorporate sectors leads to welfare losses, while shifting from direct taxation of income from capital to indirect consumption taxation leads to large gains.
Piggott	Replacement of all taxes and subsidies with an equal-yield export tax leads to a total welfare gain of 3.5 percent of NDP
Keller	Efficiency effects of most taxes are small (about 10 percent of the induced changes in public consumption); an increase in corporate income tax generates a positive excess burden that it twice the resulting change in consumption, with only a moderate burden borne by suppliers of capital.
Kehoe and Serra-Puche	Goal of stimulating activity in agriculture and foodstuffs by exempting these sectors from taxation appears plausible; all model scenarios estimate that the lowest- and highest-income household will benefit more from the tax changes considered than will the middle-income groups.
Kehoe *et al.*	Introduction of value-added tax reduces consumer welfare by 2-3 percent on average, with the high-income group experiencing greater reductions than the low-income group; retention of the value-added tax accompanied by a reduction in social security contributions paid by employers leads to an overall improvement in welfare.

Source: Whalley (1989)

Counterfactual experiments performed with the model involve cases in which the entire existing tax and subsidy system is changed, as well as cases in which only specific taxes are abolished or modified. Each counterfactual policy change is made with yield-preserving, broadly-based taxes or subsidies that keep the size of the public sector constant. Without this procedure, changes in the relative size of the public and private sectors in the model can give misleading estimates of gains or losses from tax changes, especially where the focus of the analysis is on the distorting effects of particular taxes and subsidies.

Piggott and Whalley estimated that the U.K. tax and subsidy system accounted for annual welfare losses of 6 to 9 percent of net domestic product in 1973, an estimate that at the time was higher than that conventionally thought for such distortions. They found the principal sources of these losses to be capital income taxes, excise taxes, and local authority housing subsidies, which jointly accounted for approximately 80 percent of the distorting costs of the combined tax and subsidy system. They also found the effects of inflation (in the absence of indexing) represent another significant source of distorting loss.

Income redistribution effects of the tax and subsidy system were also assessed. In welfare terms, they found that the removal of all tax and subsidy policies and their replacement by a yield-preserving single-rate commodity tax inflicted a welfare loss on the poorest decile of households equivalent to around 20 percent of their income (in part due to the removal of local authority housing subsidies), while the top decile gained about the same amount (in part through the removal of the income tax). These results differ from the conventional view of the redistributive effects of the tax system based on incidence calculations, which are still taken by many to suggest that the tax system has almost no effect on the household income distribution.[9]

Ballard *et al.* (1985) subsequently developed a related model of the U.S. economy having as its major focus intertemporal aspects of tax policy. Like Piggott and Whalley, their elasticity estimates were derived from literature sources, and they performed sensitivity analyses for the more important parameters, principally elasticities of labour supply and saving. They calculated a sequence of single-period static equilibria, in which savings decisions changed the time profile of the economy's capital stock.

Myopic expectations regarding the return on savings were assumed in order to simplify their computations, although in related work Ballard and Goulder (1985) found that a different treatment of expectations had little effect on results.

The model was used for a series of policy analyses. One was to evaluate four plans for corporate and personal income tax integration. They also considered replacing the federal personal income tax with a progressive consumption tax. In this latter model application, eight different plans were evaluated, differing in the fraction of savings treated as deductible, the fraction of dividends that were taxable, the fraction of nominal capital gains taxable at personal level, and the elimination or inclusion of preferential treatment of housing and changes in the corporate tax. This model has also subsequently been used to investigate, among other things, the relationship between tax rates and government revenue, and the effects of changes in tax treatment of foreign income.

In contrast to the above two models, Slemrod's (1985) general equilibrium tax model analyses U.S. capital income taxation issues, allowing for adjustments in the financial behaviour of households and firms in response to tax changes. A number of features distinguish Slemrod's from other general equilibrium tax models. The most important is the explicit treatment of risk. Capital owners are not affected identically by tax changes in the model since they hold different portfolios. This is because a risk-aversion parameter enters preferences and utility-maximising behaviour determines behaviour toward risk, as well as commodity demands. Changes in corporate financial policy enter the model through response on the supply side of financial asset markets to the different costs of issuance of financial assets, including taxes, with exogenous elasticity parameters determining these supply-side effects. Household tax rates are endogenous, tax-exempt bonds can be held in household portfolios, and rental and owner-occupied housing are separately distinguished.

Summers (1982) is one of the first to model explicit intertemporal equilibrium tax applications. He evaluates the welfare effects of capital income taxation using a numerical overlapping-generations life-cycle model, approximately specified to be representative of the U.S. economy. Only one sector is assumed; and hence the richness of the model lies in its intertemporal specification. One of the most important features of this model is the high interest elasticity of household savings that it generates. Summers argues that the commonly used two-period formulation of savings behaviour underestimates the interest elasticity because it ignores the wealth effect associated with changes in interest rates. Summers finds much greater implied interest elasticities of savings for almost any plausible representation of a life-cycle model than conventionally thought to be the case.

Summers uses his model to evaluate alternatives to existing capital income taxation, specifically taxation of labour income or of consumption. Using a comparison across steady states, Summers estimates that a wage tax will increase income by 14 percent, and replacing it with a consumption tax, by 18 percent. These results reflect his high interest elasticity of savings in the model, which leads to a substantial increase in capital formation.

He estimates that replacing an income tax with a wage tax in the U.S. would increase welfare by nearly 5 percent of lifetime earnings; replacing it with a consumption tax would increase welfare by approximately 12 percent, the equivalent of nearly five years' income for the economy. Summers attributes the greater gains estimated under consumption taxes to increased capital formation. He concludes from all his numerical model results that the costs of capital income taxation seem much higher than had previously been believed.

Subsequently, Goulder and Summers (1987) have formulated a different tax model of the United States in which they treat investment demand explicitly, rather than assume that it is determined by savings, as in Summers' earlier work. They also explicitly incorporate the adjustment costs faced under any reallocation of capital between industries in response to capital income tax changes, using a quadratic adjustment cost formulation, similar to that used by Treadway (1969). As a result, capitalisation effects of tax policies enter their analysis.

Goulder and Summers first evaluate a number of tax policy changes assuming that these changes are unanticipated. They calculate equilibria for their policy experiments at one-year intervals over a seventy-five-year period, with personal taxes being scaled to yield equal tax revenue in all their model simulations. Goulder and Summers conclude that the effects of tax changes shown by their policy simulations, while consistent with economic theory, would not have been obtained in models with perfect intersectoral mobility of capital or static expectations. They also point out the importance for their results of the distinction between new and existing capital in their model.

A related modelling effort is by Galper, Lucke, and Toder (1989), who extend previous work on the interactions of behaviour toward risk and taxes. They examine the effects of tax policy changes on the allocation of physical capital by industry in a model that incorporates firm and household portfolio choice under uncertainty. Their model contains an explicit treatment of risk and uncertainty. It also differs from traditional Harberger-type general equilibrium tax models in including an optimising equation for corporate debt-equity decision-making instead of assuming it is fixed. Their model also allows asset demands to differ among households.

The policy changes they examine include the introduction of a flat-rate tax for corporate and personal income and full integration of corporate and personal taxes. In implementing their experiments, Galper, Lucke, and Toder compare their model with Harberger-type (no risk or financial modelling) simulations, achieved by replacing the demand for risky assets in the full version of their model with a specification that equalises risk-adjusted returns for the representative asset holder and by fixing the corporate debt-equity ratio at its initial value. There are substantial differences in the results from the two model specifications.

The effects of tax policy changes estimated for the Harberger-type model are in some cases opposite in sign to those of the full specification model. Galper, Lucke, and Toder thus conclude that the way in which financial behaviour is modelled is an important determinant of the effects of tax changes on physical capital stock allocation among industries.

Jorgenson and Yun (1984) use an intertemporal general equilibrium model for the United States to analyse the impact of tax policies on capital allocation. Their analysis of tax issues concentrates on the provisions of U.S. tax law applicable to income from capital. Their work is distinguished by the use of econometric methods for estimating model parameters. Their estimation involves the construction of a system of accounts for the United States for 1955-80 that includes income and expenditure accounts for the business and household sectors.

Jorgenson and Yun's simulation indicate that policies with effective tax rates of zero for all assets dominate other tax reforms. Expensing of investment expenditures and elimination of sales taxes on investment goods yield the greatest potential gains: $3.6 trillion (in 1980 dollars) under a lump-sum revenue adjustment, or 43 percent of 1980 private national wealth. Under increases in labour income taxes or sales taxes, these gains are reduced to $1.9 trillion and $1.7 trillion, respectively, because of offsetting distortions.

Implications and extensions

What one concludes from all these model results inevitably remains subjective. Some people are convinced by some of them, while others are more sceptical. Some like some of the features of any given model, but find others disturbing and often attach only limited credibility to model results. Results can often reveal as much about the model structure and the key role of particular parameter values as about the economy being modelled. But fresh insights emerge that are frequently provocative and stimulate debate. They can support or contradict previously held positions or provide genuinely new perspectives (frequently where no received wisdom exists).

One of the more prominent themes emerging from the general equilibrium tax modelling work thus far concerns broad-ranging implications for the equity and efficiency effects of taxes. This is because the importance of model results has to be gauged relative to the perspectives on the equity-efficiency trade-off that prevailed before the current round of modelling. In the early 1960s beliefs about efficiency effects of taxes were largely based on Harberger's pioneering work. Harberger (1959, 1962, 1966) had estimated that the efficiency costs of the US corporate tax were perhaps one-half to three-quarters of 1 percent of GNP. In a famous paper in 1964 he extended his work to a wider analysis of the efficiency effects of the whole tax system, and his conclusion was that the major efficiency costs of distorting taxes lay in the corporate tax area, and that the combined efficiency costs of all major taxes were perhaps 1 percent of GNP. At the time, many people interpreted these estimates not in the same sense as Harberger, but rather as demonstrating that the efficiency costs of taxes were small.

Perceptions of distributional effects of taxes have long been based on tax incidence calculations that have their origins in the work of Bowley, Stamp, and Clark, and even earlier, of Gregory King. From the more recent work by Pechman and Okner (1974) and Pechman (1985) on tax burdens in the United States, the picture that has emerged is that the tax system does little to redistribute income. Their analysis suggests that there is progression in tax rates under the income tax (which is perhaps less in practice than might appear on paper) but this is offset by regression elsewhere in the tax system, such as in sales and excise taxes and payroll taxes.

In the 1960s and 1970s the belief among economists, in part influenced by these studies, seems to have been that while the tax system had repeatedly been changed in an attempt to make the tax system more redistributive, little of this change had proved successful. Since the efficiency costs of the additional interventions associated with changed tax policies appeared to be small, the direction suggested for tax policy seemed to be to continue with attempts to make the tax system more redistributive, in the hope that substantive redistribution would eventually be achieved. Meanwhile, social costs through any induced misallocation of resources would not be a major factor.

This view of the tax system has clearly been challenged by the results from the general equilibrium tax policy models. The efficiency costs of taxes reported are generally much higher than those suggested by Harberger's work, especially the costs at the margin as extra revenues are raised from existing distorting taxes. In their work in the 1970s on the U.K. tax-subsidy system, for instance, Piggott and Whalley (1985) suggest a range of between 6 and 9 percent of GNP per year for the annual welfare costs from distortions. In comparable work on the United States, Ballard, Shoven and Whalley (1985) suggest an estimate in the region of 4-7 percent of GNP. These models have also been used to calculate the efficiency costs of raising additional tax revenues by using existing distorting taxes. Ballard, Shoven and Whalley, for instance, suggest efficiency costs for the United States of around 35 cents per additional dollar of revenues collected. Ballard (1987) evaluates the efficiency costs of redistribution through the tax system.

Model results have also suggested that the redistributive effects of taxes may be more significant than those portrayed in earlier incidence studies. In part, this reflects the added price endogeneity in these models. But as pointed out by Browning (1978), fully allocating the burden of indirect taxes (such as sales and excise taxes) to purchasers of taxed commodities, as in most incidence calculations, tends to produce a less progressive pattern.

If one takes these model results seriously, the perspective they offer on the equity-efficiency choice in the design of tax policy seems to challenge earlier received wisdom. Efficiency costs of taxes appear more important than previously thought, and the tax system redistributes income to a more substantial degree. The implication is that weight should shift more toward efficiency considerations and away from redistributive issues in tax design.

Policy relevant insights also emerge from general equilibrium tax policy models assessing the relative importance of inter-asset and intertemporal tax distortions. Hamilton and Whalley (1985) for instance, highlight how a Haig-Simons approach toward tax reform stresses the need to fully include imputed housing income in the tax base on the grounds that this is part of broadly-based income. However, when the issue of tax treatment of housing is approached from a consumption tax point of view, housing income appears to be appropriately taxed; it is the income return to non-housing assets that seems to be inappropriately treated. But, as Hamilton and Whalley point out, tax breaks for housing occur only if owners of housing directly consume the services yielded by the asset. There is therefore both an intertemporal and an inter-asset distortion involved in evaluating the effects of the current tax treatment of housing. The model uses 1972 data for Canada to simulate the effects of either removing taxes on other assets, or including housing income in the tax base. They show that a move from the current tax treatment to either a pure income tax or a pure consumption tax is welfare improving. These results are consistent with the themes emerging from the work by King and Fullerton (1984) and others on effective tax rates, which have also stressed the importance of inter-asset tax distortions. These results thus suggest that the variance of tax treatment across assets is a more important source of distortion than conventional intertemporal tax distortions.

Both of these examples illustrate the ability of general equilibrium tax policy models to provide important insights into policy issues. Some are generated by applying an existing model to an issue for which there were no previous results. Others reflect insights from quantification in a general equilibrium framework capturing price endogeneity.

Qualifications

Although important insights have been generated by these models, there are remaining shortcomings with existing models that both weaken the impact of results and make some modellers cautious about promoting their models too vigorously. One key problem is in selecting the appropriate treatment for the taxes to be studied. Any tax evaluated with a general equilibrium model has to be represented in some model-equivalent form, and a specification of tax rates is needed in order to complete the model. The formulation adopted has important implications for the behaviour of these models and, to a degree, predetermines results.

A number of examples serve to illustrate this point. For instance, there has been debate for some years on whether the property tax is an excise tax or a tax on factor incomes. A series of different treatments of the corporate tax have been offered since Harberger's original treatment of it as a partial factor tax. Stiglitz (1973) suggested that the corporate tax should be considered as a lump-sum tax. More recent literature has focused on the tax as applying to equity financing by firms. King and Fullerton (1984) and others have also emphasised how the effective tax rates on corporations vary and have to be disaggregated to a fine level of detail to capture their marginal effects, even to the level at which project investment decisions are made. In their analysis, effective tax rates depend upon the financing vehicle used, eligibility for investment tax credits, loss carry-forwards, and many other features.

Elasticities also represent an area of difficulty, in part because the empirical literature is not conclusive as to what are appropriate elasticity values. The problem is more difficult than just selecting elasticity values, because the ways in which model parameters are generated from literature elasticities also involve pitfalls. Two of the more important sets of elasticities used illustrate the difficulties: elasticities of labour supply, and elasticities of savings with respect to the real net-of-tax rate of return on capital. In both cases there is substantial ambiguity in the literature about the appropriate elasticity values.

A further difficulty is in choosing the appropriate level of commodity and industry aggregation. On the one hand, the level of aggregation should be kept small, to generate clearer intuition as to the ways in which the model behaves, to keep execution costs within manageable bounds, and to keep the data requirements of the model modest. On the other hand, claims to realism and the pressures from the policy process will often dictate more detailed aggregation. The more detailed general equilibrium tax models have around thirty to forty commodities. But even this is some way from the level of detail at which tax policy makers typically operate. For household disaggregation, Slemrod (1985) uses micro unit data in general equilibrium tax models, the most ambitious attempt at disaggregation thus far, but, as Slemrod notes, this comes with a significant computational cost.

Yet another problem area is the process through which models are calibrated. In most cases this involves calibrating a chosen model structure to a given benchmark equilibrium data set. This method has caused some discomfort, especially to econometricians. This is because under calibration the numerical specification produced for any given model is not tested in any meaningful statistical sense. Econometricians who would like to see calibration applied to more than a single data observation have suggested system-wide estimation of models (see Mansur and Whalley, 1984).

A further source of discomfort with present tax models is the widespread use of convenient functional forms, such as Cobb-Douglas, CES, and LES. Recent econometric literature rejects the strong separability assumptions implicit in CES functions. Some have therefore suggested that more flexible functional forms should be used in these models, but as yet little work has been done using functions such as the translog because they may not behave well for large changes.

Most of the applied modellers who have dealt with tax policy issues have also confronted important issues of model closure, that is, the need to close off models in some way to features not central to the question being analysed. The problem is that while a feature may not appear crucial for the issue under analysis, the closure treatment adopted may nonetheless have substantial effects on the behaviour of the model

Take for instance foreign trade. Should the model assume the economy is a price taker or price maker on world markets? And if the economy is a maker of prices, how should one specify the behaviour of trading partners? Other closure issues are the treatment of investment and savings, and the treatment of government expenditures and public goods and transfers.

A final issue of model design concerns the balance between issue-specific and general-purpose modelling. In the early work done in the 1970s with the general equilibrium tax models, the focus was very much on building general-purpose models that yielded the capability to analyse several different taxes simultaneously. While these models have been helpful in providing an overall assessment of how tax systems operate, their weaknesses have increasingly become apparent as they have been used for specific policy analyses. For the analysis of particular policy questions, model users often find that there is unnecessary detail in these models, yet the model treatment and detail relevant to the policy question at hand is frequently not wholly satisfactory. Model users have often had to modify parts of existing models while carrying along significant amounts of excess baggage in order to be relevant to the policy questions being examined. The reaction to this in more recent modelling work has been to focus on more issue-specific, targeted modelling. However, issue-specific models also have their weaknesses. It is easy to repeatedly reconstruct models that are so closely related that it is an inefficient exercise. Also, these models miss many of the policy and other interactions captured in a general-purpose model. And while many of these effects may be of secondary importance for the issue at hand, the difficulty is that, *ex ante*, it is never wholly apparent which effects are more important. A virtue of a large general-purpose model is that by taking a first cut at a policy issue one obtains some indication as to which feedback elements are important for subsequent further development.

Experiences with general equilibrium tax policy modelling clearly demonstrates the need to be able to work simultaneously on several levels. Modellers need to have a good grasp of economic theory, a sense of the policy issues they are working on, familiarity with computers, an ability to interpret and communicate their results, and a full understanding of the data with which they are working. This suggests the need for modelling teams, the direction taken in other areas, particularly the natural sciences.

No doubt this is a direction research in the tax area will take as it focuses more fully on the policy questions of the day.

3.2 Environmental Models

The natural environment, and the degradation thereof, has been a focus of interest for economic analysis for some considerable length of time. Pigovian analysis is well suited to evaluating appropriate instruments for dealing with externalities. Until comparatively recently, however, it could not be said to be anywhere near the top of the research agenda. Growing public concern with the consequences of environmental degradation have driven the issue firmly on to the political agenda. This reinforced a growing interest in the research community. It is now a major research theme in the UK and elsewhere. "Environmental Economics" now encompasses a broad range of issues relating to: global warming; optimal depletion rates of natural resources; international spillovers; the interface between environmental and other policies, (most notably trade policies); sustainable development; and endangered species.

Here we confine our attention to various issues in the economics of global warming. Despite the considerable degree of scientific ignorance about the phenomenon more progress has been made here than in other areas, with attention being directed primarily at the costs and benefits of global warming, the costs of alternative abatement policies, and the interface between abatement costs and trade policies. CGE techniques have been deployed to analyse these issues. Moreover, alternative modelling strategies have also been utilised. Comprehensive surveys have been completed by Boero, Clarke and Winters (1991), Cline (1991) and Hoeller, Dean and Hayafuji (1992).

Overview of key models

Table 3.3 summarises the features of the principal global warming/carbon tax models. One of the most ambitious models is that developed by Burniaux *et al.* (1992a, 1992b) - the OECD General Equilibrium Environmental Model, more widely known as GREEN. It is a multi-region, multi-sector CGE model, built for purposes of comparing alternative policies directed at curbing CO_2 emissions. The model has 11 production sectors, and a single representative consumer. Production functions are Leontief or

CES, with imperfect substitutability between old and new capital goods, to facilitate the incorporation of adjustment costs. The coverage of this model is four OECD regions and eight non-OECD, all of which are linked by bilateral trade matrices. A variety of sources of fossil fuels are incorporated, with appropriate backstop technologies. Dynamics are captured by a recursive structure which is driven by capital accumulation and the depletion of natural resources. Simulations are run over 5 or 25 year intervals and the policy instruments evaluated are a carbon tax, an energy tax, and trade in emission rights.

TABLE 3.3 MAIN CHARACTERISTICS OF ENVIRONMENTAL CGE MODELS

Model	*Economies Studied*	*Base Year*	*Time Period*	*Dimensionality*	*Policies Covered*	*Functional Forms*
Burniaux *et al.* (1992)	12 Regions	1985	1985-2050	• 11 Production Sectors • Representative consumer	• Carbon tax • energy tax • trade in emission rights	Leontief and CES functions
Whalley and Wigle (1989)	3 Regions	1986	1990-2030	• 3 traded goods • 2 non-traded goods	• national production based tax • national consumption based tax • global tax	Nested CES functions
Perroni and Rutherford (1991)	5 Regions		-2020	•2 Production Sectors		
Rutherford (1992)	5 Regions	1990	1990-2100	• 2 Production Sectors	• Carbon tax	CES
Jorgenson and Wilcoxen (1990)	United States		1990-2060	•35 Production Sectors • 672 Household types • 4 Factors	• Emissions freeze • carbon tax • energy tax	Econometric-ally estimated production functions
Blitzer *et al.* (1990)	Egypt	1987	1987-2052	• 10 Production Sectors		Fixed coefficient
Glomsrød *et al.* (1990)	Norway		2000-2010	•31 Production Sectors		

This is a large dimension model which is richer in its specification than many others. From the standpoint of modelling CO_2 abatement it has a number of distinctive features. The microeconomic underpinnings are well developed and both the production and consumption sectors are transparent. The consistent treatment of world trade linkages, the incorporation of adjustment costs and the explicit modelling of exhaustible resources are also desirable characteristics. Given the nature of the problem being evaluated, the facility to run simulations which facilitate comparisons of alternative policy instruments and investigate the distributional consequences of alternative scenarios is a major asset.

Equally however, the model inevitably draws attention to many of the key problems with CGE modelling. For example, forward-looking behaviour is not well represented, with agents assumed to be myopic. Intertemporal accumulation is modelled in a fairly mechanistic fashion - although it must be said that this is not peculiar to CGE modelling. Finally, given the fact that this is a large dimension model, there are inevitably a large number of exogenous variables to be parameterised.

A somewhat smaller scale, and less ambitious, model is that of Whalley and Wigle (1989). The motivation behind this is partly to assess the costs of various carbon tax options, and their distributional consequences globally, and partly to explore the interface between environmental and trade policies. The model embraces three regions - developed countries, developing countries and oil exporters, which produce five commodities, two non-traded and three traded. Some of the products are energy intensive, and some are not. The objective of intervention is to reduce global carbon usage by 50% relative to the base case (calibrated to 1986). This can be accomplished by a national production based tax, a national consumption based tax, or a global tax. For the world as a whole, the total cost of carbon taxes (measured in terms of equivalent variation), is around 2% of global GDP. Interestingly however there are very substantial differences across regions, depending to the type of instruments used. Thus, developing countries lose 4% of GDP under a national production-based tax, but gain 3% under a global tax; developed countries lose much more under a global tax than under a national-based consumption tax, (because of revenue effects); oil exporters clearly gain from a national production-based tax, but lose from the others.

TABLE 3.4 POLICY IMPLICATIONS OF RESULTS FROM MODELS SUMMARISED IN TABLE 3.3.

Model	**Policy Implications**
Burniaux *et al*. (1992)	Wide regional variation in carbon tax levels and welfare losses. Welfare losses from carbon taxes of up to 2% of GDP. International agreements on trade in emission rights leads to welfare improvement
Whalley and Wigle (1989)	Mid range losses from carbon taxes of 2% of GDP. Wide regional variations in costs depending upon the tax instrument used. Different environmental regulations across countries likely to create pressures on trade policies.
Jorgenson and Wilcoxen (1990)	Comparatively low losses from carbon taxes of 0.2% to 1.1% of GDP. Modest non-energy intersectoral adjustment. Carbon tax more efficient than alternatives. Costs of emission controls higher in developing than developed countries
Blitzer *et al.* (1990)	Relatively high losses from emission reductions, of 4.3% to 22% of baseline welfare. Intersectoral adjustments away from manufacturing and energy intensive activity, towards agriculture and services.
Rutherford (1992)	Global loss in GDP of 3.6% relative to baseline, by 2100. GDP losses higher for industrialised than less industrialised countries. Potential for welfare gains from trade in emissions rights.

Despite the relative simplicity of this model it draws attention directly to the global distributional consequences of intervention. In the context of global warming this is a crucial consideration and a potentially important source of policy conflict. As Whalley (1991) argues, this not only makes the choice of instrument very important, it also points up the scope which exists for trade policies being deployed to enforce environmental policy, and the potential for contingency measures (like anti-dumping rules) to complicate the picture further.

Jorgenson and Wilcoxen (1990) is a country-specific model, but one which is on a relatively large scale with 35 production sectors, 672 household types and 4 factors of production. The model has a number of distinctive characteristics. Unusually, perhaps even uniquely for a CGE model, its parameters are not calibrated but estimated from time series data. The model itself has full factor mobility and assumes rational optimising agents with perfect foresight. It is used to evaluate the consequences of a freeze on emissions and a reduction in emissions to 80% of their 1990 level. GDP losses associated with the carbon taxes required to hit these targets range from 0.2% to 0.1% of GDP. As can be seen from the summary of results in Table 3.4, these are relatively low losses when compared with the output of other models which seems to be driven largely by the full factor mobility assumption. Intersectoral output reallocations are relatively modest outside the energy sector.

Two other outcomes from the Jorgenson-Wilcoxen model are notable, (if not wholly surprising). First they experiment with alternative forms of intervention and find that the costs of a carbon tax are lower than those associated with either a general energy tax or a general *ad valorem* tax. This is precisely what optimal intervention analysis would predict. Second, the costs of emission controls are considerably higher in developing than in developed countries. This results from the fact that developing countries start from much lower baseline emissions than developed countries.

Thus, although Jorgenson and Wilcoxen is a single country study, it is one which has a rich specification and some genuinely novel features. It suggests that the costs of curbing greenhouse gases are likely to be somewhat lower than many other studies, and the process of adjustment to an emission regime somewhat smoother.

Blitzer, Eckaus, Lahiri and Meeraus (1990) build and compute a CGE model for Egypt. The model has four energy sectors and six non-energy sectors and is therefore relatively large in scale. Unlike many other models the production sector has a fixed coefficient rather than CES structure, with capital specific to each sector. A range of emission cutbacks are investigated, from 25% to 40%. These result in falls in baseline welfare of 4.4% to 22%. These relatively high losses appear to be driven by the fixed coefficients/sector specific capital structure which imposes high adjustment costs.

Rutherford (1992) is a dynamic general equilibrium model which is based on the same data set as Manne and Richels (1991). Unlike the latter however, it explicitly incorporates world trade flows. Its time horizon is 1990 to 2100. It is a five region model (US, other OECD, China, former Soviet Union and the rest of the world). Carbon taxes are used as the instrument of emissions reduction, but an effective ceiling on the tax is placed by inclusion of a carbon free backstop technology. Moreover, an autonomous energy improvement is also built into the model, (the magnitude of which initially varies across regions according to their stage of industrialisation). The global loss in GDP associated with a carbon tax amounts to 3.6%, relative to base line, by 2100. This is in fact relatively low by comparison with other models - an outcome which is determined by autonomous energy improvement and the availability of a backstop technology. As in other models, there is a considerable dispersion around this estimate, from 1.5% for OECD countries (excluding the US), through to 4.5% for the rest of the world.

Difference in model outputs

As can be seen from the foregoing overview, there are marked differences between the output of many of these models. Moreover, there are important differences in structure, and output, between the CGE models and alternatives like dynamic optimising models (e.g. Manne and Richels (1990a), Peck and Teisberg (1990)), and the multi-sector macro models (e.g. Bye *et al.* (1989), Nagata *et al.* (1991)). We will consider the contrasts between CGE optimising and dynamic optimising models shortly. For the moment we focus on the differences in model outcomes reported in Table 3.5.

We saw in Chapter 2 that CGE models can have rich and complicated structures. The final form which a model takes depends in part on the objectives of the modeller, and in part on the availability of data. We can see from Table 3.3 that dimensionality varies considerably across studies. Some are relatively simple two sector models, others have a large number of production sectors; some are single country, others are multi-country; some explicitly model trade flows, most do not; and most have different starting points with respect to initial energy prices. Clearly these structural features will have an impact on model outcomes. We also saw in Chapter 2 however that the process of parameterisation/calibration, and the dynamics imposed are invariably model specific, and will have a crucial bearing on model outcomes. In the context of environmental models, the elasticities of substitution assumed between energy and non-energy inputs will have a critical impact on the responsiveness of output to an abatement intervention. As Hoeller *et al.* (1992) show, the range of estimates deployed is quite wide.

TABLE 3.5 GROWTH EFFECT OF CO_2 EMISSION REDUCTION

Global Models	**Change in growth rate of GDP**	**End-year GDP as a percent of baseline**	**Carbon tax ($/ton carbon) (end-year)**
Oliveira-Martins *et al.* (1992)	-0.0	-2.6	230
Manne/Richels (1990b)			
USA	-0.0	-2.5	
Other OECD	-0.0	-1.8	
Eastern Europe	-0.0	-2.5	-250
China	-0.1	-10.5	
Rest of World	-0.0	-4.0	
Whalley/Wigle (1991) (3)			
National producer taxes	..	-4.4(4)	462.8
National consumer taxes	..	-2.1(4)	463.1
Global tax	..	-4.2(4)	459.7
Ceiling on *per-capita* emissions	..	-8.5(4)	..
Cline (1989)	-0.1	-7.4	..
Mintzer (1987)	-0.0	-3.0	..
IEA (1990) (5)			
Carbon tax scenario	-0.2	..	72
70% nuclear plus carbon tax scenario	-0.2	..	72
Nordhaus (1991a and 1991b)			
Low	-0.0	..	48.5
Middle	-0.0	..	119.0
High	-0.1	..	..
Nordhaus (1991a)			
Rapid phase-in scenario	-0.3 (7)	..	..
Rapid phase-in using regulation	-0.5(7)	..	..
Edmonds/Barns (1990)	-0.2	-8.0	436.5
Perroni/Rutherford (1991)		-1.0	

TABLE 3.5 continued

Country-specific Results:	**Change in growth rate of GDP**	**End-year GDP as a percent of baseline**	**Carbon tax ($/ton carbon) (end-year)**
Manne/Richels (1990a, USA)			
a) technology pessimistic case	-0.1	-4.0	-250 (2100)
b) technology intermediate case	-0.0	-2.5	..
c) technology optimistic case	-0.0	-0.8	..
CBO (1990, USA)			
DRI model	-0.2	-2.0	100
DGEM	-0.1	-0.6	100
Jorgenson/ Wilcoxen (1991, USA)	..	-0.3	7 (2020)
	..	-0.5	17 (2020)
	..	-1.6	60 (2020)
Goulder (1991, USA)	..	-1.0	25
	..	-2.2	50
	..	-4.5	100
Blitzer *et al.*, (1990, Egypt)			
Scenario 1	-0.1	-2.7	..
Scenario 3	-1.0	-15.00	..
Scenario 5	-1.5	-19.0	..
Glomsrød *et al.* (1990, Norway)	-0.4	2.7	..
Bye *et al.* (1989, Norway) (2000)	-1.0 to -0.2	-1 to -2	..
NEPP (1989, Netherlands) (2)			
National policy scenario (2010)	-0.2	-4.2	..
Global policy scenario (2010)	0.0	0.6	..
Bergman (1990, Sweden) (2000)	-0.4	-5.56	..
Dixon *et al.* (1989, Australia)	-0.1	-2.4	..
Proost/Regemorter (1990, Belgium)	..	-1.8	315 (2010)
Christensen (1991, Finland)			
Unilateral action	-0.4	-6.9	..
Global action	-0.3	-4.8	..
DRI (1991, EC) (4)	-0.1	-0.8	80 (2005)
Nagata *et al.* (1991, Japan)	-0.3	-4.9	492 (2005)
Ban (1991, Japan)			
Tax Case	..	-0.4(5)	..
Regulation case	..	-1.7(5)	..

Source: adapted from Dean and Hoeller (1992)

Most of the CGE model simulations are for a relatively long time period. Assumptions made with respect to technical progress, adjustment and expectations are therefore very important in determining model outcomes. The first of these is arguably the most important, but is also rather difficult to model. Some like Whalley and Wigle (1989) ignore it completely; others incorporate it via some backstop technology which is assumed to come on stream at some date in the future (e.g. Rutherford 1992 and Oliveira Martins *et al.* 1992). Related to the issue of whether a backstop is incorporated is the question of the speed at which the system adjusts to emission controls. As Nordhaus (1991a) shows, rapid implementation of emission controls could generate relatively high adjustment costs resulting from premature scrapping of the capital stock. Different models assume different adjustment paths and this too influences results.

Finally, since we are dealing with an intertemporal adjustment problem, the manner in which expectations are formulated, and updated, will have an impact on outcomes. Most models assume static expectations, although Jorgenson and Wilcoxen (1991) and Blitzer *et al.* (1990) assume rational expectations. Given the time frame over which the analyses are being conducted, neither is ideal, with the former being especially inappropriate. The key point is that results are sensitive to the expectations regime assumed.

Contrasts between CGE and Dynamic Optimising Models

As we have seen, there is quite a range of results generated by CGE models, and in the previous sub-section we discussed the key reasons for these differences. As can also be seen from Table 3.5 there is a considerable range of outcomes across CGE and dynamic optimising models. In an attempt to disentangle the source of variation as between differences in model structure, and differences in baseline and reduction scenarios, Dean and Hoeller (1992) attempt to standardise baseline scenarios and reduction strategies across six models - three of which are CGE, two have a dynamic optimising structure, and one is an econometric energy model. These are: Rutherford (1992), Oliveira Martins *et al* . (1992), Whalley and Wigle (1992), Barns *et al* . (1992), Manne and Richels (1991) and Venyoukas (1992). The key points which Dean and Hoeller identify are as follows. First, terminal emissions vary considerably, from 22.5 billion tons to 65 billion tons in 2100 on a "business as usual" assumption. This is attributable to differences across the models in what they assume about the rate of autonomous energy improvement, as well as future emissions. For example, Whalley and Wigle assume no autonomous energy efficiency improvement and, with only two energy sources, have limited scope for substitution. Both energy improvement and emissions paths require judgements about the rate of technical progress. These judgements are independent of model structure.

The carbon taxes required to secure a given abatement level vary considerably across models. The key source of diversity here seems to be what is built in regarding backstop technologies. Some models build in carbon-free backstops which are assumed to come on stream at some specified date. When they do, they effectively place an upper limit on the carbon tax required. Incorporation of a backstop scenario is not model specific - both CGE and optimising models can include them, (e.g. both Manne and Richels, and Burniaux *et al.* do so). Growth effects also show considerable diversity due in part to the differences in carbon tax paths, and the assumed distribution of emissions across countries. Again these are differences which are not attributable to CGE *vis-à-vis* optimising structures, but rather the underlying economic structure. Other sources of differences in output are the substitution possibilities assumed, the composition of energy demand built in, and the possibilities for emissions trading. The first and second have a crucial bearing on differences in taxes and costs which are required, the third can impact significantly on the regional distribution of abatement costs.

If most of the differences in results are attributable to inputs rather than differences in model structure, are there any advantages from a modelling standpoint, of relying on CGE *vis-à-vis* dynamic optimising models, one way or the other? Typically, the optimising models (DOMs) are energy specific, whereas the CGE models adopt a more macroeconomic/international trade perspective. This generally means that the DOMs have a more disaggregated structure, and rely to a much greater extent on econometrically estimated rather than calibrated coefficients. Given their dynamic structure, DOMs also tend to incorporate a wider menu of technological options, and are estimated over a longer time horizon. Since the phenomenon being investigated is one where long run effects are important, this is a desirable feature. The other important attribute of their dynamic structure is that, in contrast to CGE models, they can yield dynamic paths. Not only does this facilitate more thorough investigation of adjustment processes, it also offers a framework for incorporating technical change and endogenous shocks more readily.

CGE models also have some desirable features however. The fact that they are built from a macro/trade perspective allows international linkages to be better modelled. Moreover, it also facilitates a much more thorough assessment of the distributional consequences of various interventions. Finally CGE models offer the facility for assessing welfare changes by reference to a welfare measure, rather than just in terms of a change in GDP.

Overall, CGE models and DOMs have complementary attributes - the former offer a more suitable structure for addressing long run consequences; the latter are better suited to identifying short run/distributional changes associated with abatement policies. Having said that, we have to acknowledge that there are very real problems with *any* modelling in this field. There is considerable scientific uncertainty regarding the path of emissions, and the damage that emissions may be causing; considerable technical uncertainty with respect to the potential for autonomous energy improvements, the development of backstop technologies and the substitution possibilities across fuel sources; and of course the analysis is being conducted over a very long time frame. Inevitably these place a fairly large question mark against the reliability of any point estimates. This does not mean to say that there is no role whatsoever for modelling in this field - it is clearly important to analyse the factors responsible for differences in model outputs. It means however that we have to treat the results with caution.

3.3 Trade and Integration Studies

In the late 1970s and early 1980s the development of CGE trade models was concentrated on the construction of large multi-purpose models, either country-specific (for example, the Dixon *et al.* (1982) model of Australia) or of the world economy (such as the Whalley (1985) 4 and 7-bloc models and the Deardorff and Stern (1986)

34-country model). More recent work has concentrated on the development of smaller models that focus on specific issues, such as sectoral liberalisation (e.g. Trela and Whalley (1990) on the MFA), on trade policy when there is imperfect competition (e.g. Harris and Cox (1984) on Canadian trade liberalisation), current and capital account interactions (for example, Goulder and Eichengreen (1989)), and on dynamic models (such as the VEMOD model of Haaland *et al.* (1988)).

This section concentrates on the development of CGE models designed to address two major issues in trade policy:

- global trade liberalisation, either in multi-sectoral form (as in GATT negotiations) or sectoral-specific (for example the reform of the MFA);
- regional integration most notably the enlargement of the EC and the formation of NAFTA.

Running through the modelling of both these issues are several themes, in particular deviations from the standard perfectly competitive, homogeneous products, comparative static framework that comes from the Ricardo-Heckscher-Ohlin tradition. The most important of these themes is the developments that have been made in modelling and analysing trade policy in a world where there is 'cross-hauling', where some goods at least are differentiated or at least some sectors are imperfectly competitive. The results of modelling trade policy under such conditions have suggested that the gains to be obtained from global liberalisation and from regional integration may be substantially greater than had been suggested by perfectly competitive formulations. The approaches used in such modelling have not however escaped criticism, the most important of which is that the assumptions made largely determine the results obtained. Other themes, so far less well developed in the literature, are those of appropriately incorporating policy instruments other than taxes and subsidies within models, modelling international capital flows, and making CGE trade models dynamic, so that they can capture growth aspects.

Overview of key models

The early CGE trade models, of the late 1970s and early 1980s, although differing in their objectives and in their specifics, basically share a similar approach. All are fundamentally based on the Heckscher-Ohlin formulation, seeking to model trade flows as essentially inter-industry and explicable in terms of differing relative factor endowments. Nevertheless, all differ from the 'pure' Heckscher-Ohlin approach in certain ways.

A major deviation from the formal Heckscher-Ohlin model is forced upon CGE modellers by the need to calibrate their country-specific models to benchmark data sets for the country in question. Generally it is impossible to maintain in practice the H-O assumption that countries share a common technology, even if the same functional form is deemed appropriate. For the same reason, the assumption of common tastes, often made in the 'hard' version of the H-O model, must be violated in applied analyses. A further deviation from standard trade theory is that imported and domestically-produced goods are not assumed to be perfect substitutes. This reflects the empirical observation that much international trade, particularly between developed market economies, is intra-industry rather than inter-industry in nature. This may be explained by abandoning the standard trade-modelling assumption of perfect competition, and replacing it with a variety of assumptions about product differentiation, scale economies and market structure. However, an alternative approach commonly taken is to assume that all markets are atomistically competitive in form, but that products are differentiated (in the eyes of the consumer) by their country of origin.

This so-called Armington approach is now an essential component of most trade models,[10] not least because it allows for a more exact calibration of models to exogenously estimated trade elasticities, and arguably a richer formulation. The use of the Armington assumption has been criticised on various grounds: that it encourages calibration to trade elasticities that are arguably too low, thus ensuring that nearly all countries have a degree of power over their terms of trade; and that it is a way of side-tracking the issue of cross-hauling rather than tackling it explicitly by modelling some or all industries as imperfectly competitive producers of heterogeneous goods. It is still a subject of debate whether some of the effects obtained in trade models making the Armington assumption are a consequence of that assumption rather than a reflection of reality (see Brown (1988)).

The other major deviation from the strict neo-classical tradition is in the form of closure adopted. Although some (such as Whalley (1985)) adhere to the Walrasian tradition, others have used a macro closure with exchange rates able to have real effects on the behaviour of the model (e.g. Deardorff and Stern (1986)), and yet in others labour markets that do not clear (as in, for example, Deardorff and Stern (1986) and some of the model variants produced by Dixon *et al.* (1982)). Otherwise, global models basically follow the standard international trade format. They are single period, and assume that markets are perfectly competitive. They embody at least two sectors, in each of which the final good is produced by the combination of one or more factors (some possibly sector-specific), and often embody intermediate products.

The original Whalley and Deardorff and Stern global models were constructed for the analysis of various tariff-cutting options that were under discussion in the GATT Tokyo Round. A schematic outline of the Whalley (1985) four-region model used for this purpose is given in Figure 3.1. This takes as its regions the US, EC and Japan and the rest of the world. Parameters for the first three are derived from region-specific data for 1973; the rest of the world is modelled 'schematically', with parameters derived as arithmetic averages of comparable parameters in the three major trading areas. There are 33 domestic commodities in each of the regions, four of which are non-traded. There is a rich specification of household groups, with 10 different household types in the US and 16 in Japan, both stratified by income, and 9 in the EC, one for each of the then members (but with Belgium and Luxembourg considered as one). Demand is specified as 2-level nested CES, form, and the value-added production functions as the CES, with fixed coefficients for intermediate inputs. The Armington assumption is made, with aggregation of imported and domestically-produced goods also through a CES function. Domestic and trade taxes and subsidies are modelled explicitly, and non-tariff barriers are represented in *ad valorem* equivalent form. The model is well-suited to the analysis of issues affecting the three specified major trading areas, but is less satisfactory for analysing the effects of policy changes on the rest of the world, and in particular the less developed countries.

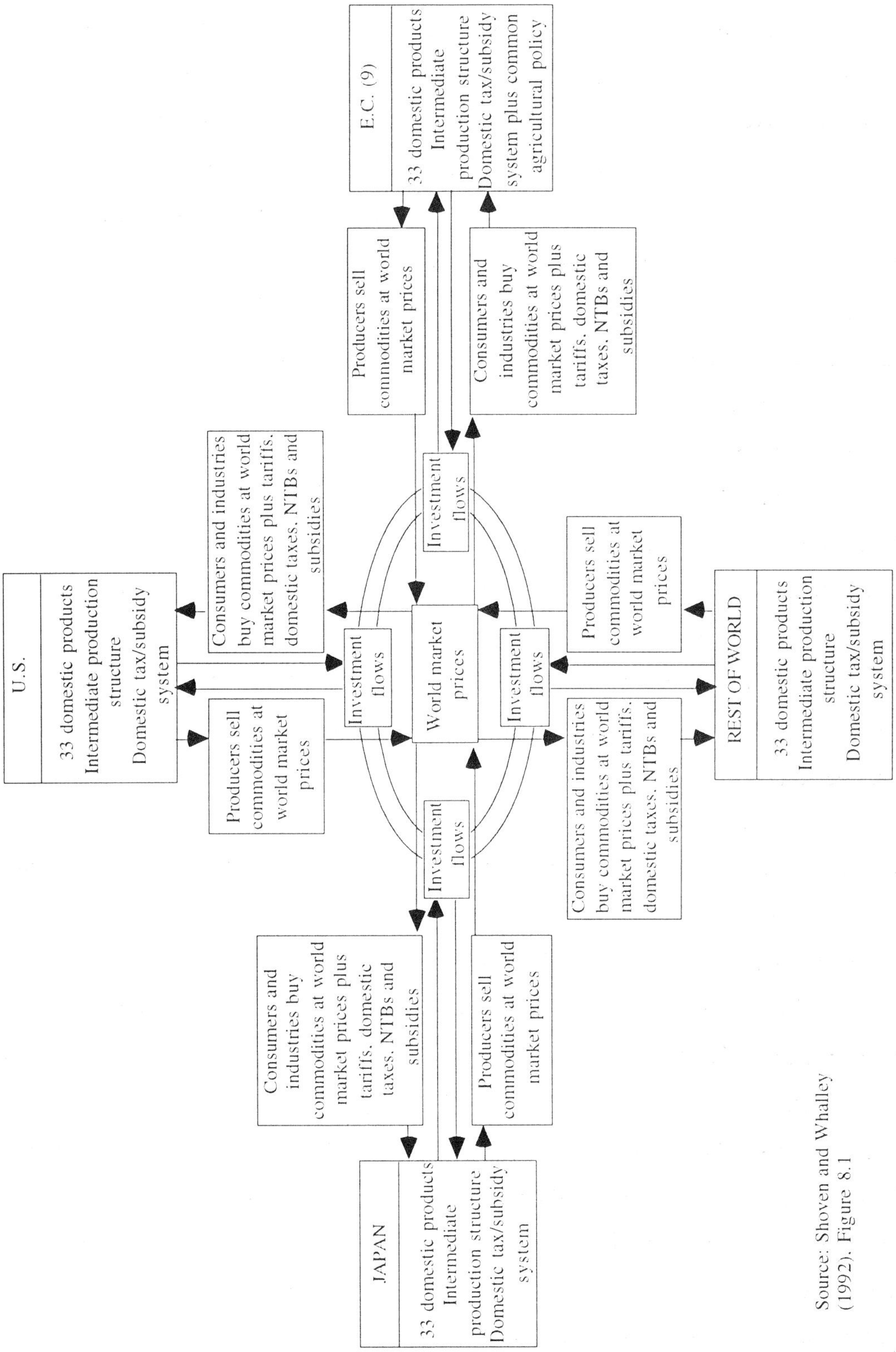

Figure 3.1: The Whalley four-sector CGE model

Whalley used this model to analyse the effects on welfare and the terms of trade for each group of seven alternative tariff-cutting formulae proposed in the Tokyo Round negotiations. His conclusion was that in general the US would make relatively smaller gains than the EC under each of the proposed formulae, and that the rest of the world would always lose. The low US gains reflect the fact that it is a major exporter of agricultural commodities while the Tokyo negotiations were concentrated on reducing protection in manufactures.

As noted above, the Whalley four-region model is not well-suited to examination of the effects of trade liberalisation on the less-developed countries (the 'North-South' issue) since these are incorporated into the 'rest of the world'. Whalley therefore developed a further model in which the world was split into seven regions, the US, EC and Japan, other developed countries, OPEC, newly industrialised countries, and less developed countries. In order to keep the model tractable it considers only 6 commodities and one representative consumer in each region. The specification of demand functions is however more detailed than in the four-region model, with household preferences modelled as a four-level nested function which incorporates both CES and LES forms.

Whalley concludes that the abolition of tariffs and non-tariff barriers in the North would result in an annual welfare gain for the LDCs and NICs of approximately $30 billion, with most of the global gain going to those two groups. An improvement in the terms of trade of the NICs and LDCs is a major factor in this. The annual gain to the 'South' from the removal of protection is about 50% greater than the annual flow of aid. Removal of trade barriers in the South would, in contrast, yield substantial gains to the North (some $80 billion) but also major losses to the South (of about $60 billion).

Nguyen, Perroni and Wigle (1991) use a CGE model to inform our understanding of the consequences of a successful conclusion to the Uruguay Round of multilateral trade negotiations (MTNs). They are not the first to use a CGE model for this purpose, Brown and Whalley (1980), Whalley (1982) and Stern (1979) having previously done so for the Tokyo Round. They are however, the first to undertake a serious CGE analysis of the Uruguay Round. Their model has nine production sectors and ten country groupings and is implemented using MPS/GE. They experiment with two possible agreements - a comprehensive outcome, and a 'face-saving' outcome. The former involves significant cuts in tariffs, agricultural support measures, non-tariff barriers, (including liberalisation of the MFA), as well as an imputed value to proxy the benefits of liberalisation in services. The face-saving agreement assumes a similar level of tariff liberalisation but more modest changes elsewhere. Net welfare benefits are calculated, and amount to $119 billion globally for the face-saving agreement, and $262 billion for the comprehensive agreement. Both the total gains, and induced changes in employment, vary considerably by country grouping.

This work illustrates nicely some of the limitations of the CGE approach, but also its strengths. The model is static, and as such misses completely the potential growth impact of a Uruguay Round settlement. Moreover, since it assumes constant returns to scale it almost certainly misses important scale benefits. However, it does provide a plausible basis for assessing outcomes, and of course does so *ex ante*. The commodity and country disaggregation facilitate a commentary on the cross-country/cross-commodity breakdown of employment and welfare changes. It is unlikely that any alternative modelling strategy could provide this kind of output.

A conclusion common to all the global models grounded in the standard trade framework is that, irrespective of the countries examined and of the details of the model specification, the effects of changes in trade policy on overall economic efficiency are relatively small. For example, the Whalley (1985) study suggested that in the worst possible case considered, in which a retaliatory trade war between the large developed country blocs led to tariffs as high as 150%, the decline in world GDP would be no more than three per cent.

The early models, both global and country-specific, also agree in predicting that policy changes would result in terms-of-trade effects that were large compared to the changes in the deadweight gain (or loss). These conclusions are tied in with the use of the Armington assumption, which allows the modeller to calibrate to exogenously estimated trade elasticities. They suggest that the levels of protection to which the models are calibrated are substantially below that which would maximise national welfare in the absence of retaliation (the 'optimum tariff'), so that a unilateral reduction in protection would make a country (or group of countries) worse off. For example,

Whalley's analysis of North-South trade suggested that the simultaneous elimination of trade restrictions by the developing countries would reduce their welfare. Such results are at such variance with the prior beliefs of policy practitioners that they have been taken as grounds for rejecting the models. The conventional wisdom holds that increases in trade had been central to world-wide growth in incomes in the post-war years, and the standard policy prescription for the developing countries is that they should liberalise their trade policies.

Nevertheless, some of the apparently paradoxical outcomes generated by these early CGE trade models did, perhaps because they could be rationalised, engender a positive reaction from policy makers. For example, the Brown and Whalley (1980) analysis of tariff-cutting proposals in the Tokyo Round suggested that countries would gain least from their own tariff cutting proposals. Thus, the EC stood to make the greatest gain if the US proposal of a linear cut was adopted, since the EC was a net exporter of manufactures to the US. The EC however was arguing for a non-linear harmonising tariff-cutting procedure. In a similar vein, the Miller and Spencer (1977) analysis of the effects on the UK of joining the EC showed that the major determinant of whether it would gain or lose lay not in the traditional trade creation versus trade diversion trade-off, but in the size of the UK's contribution to the EC budget. Such outcomes from CGE trade models have often forced decision makers to re-examine the logic of their policy stance.

Concern with the outcomes of these early models, and the belief that such outcomes were strongly dependent on their structure, generated much discussion. Criticisms may be considered under five headings:

- the scarcity of, and lack of mutual consistency in, estimated demand, supply and trade elasticities, and the often crude assumptions that had to be made when working with large multi-country data sets;
- the use of the Armington assumption to account for intra-industry trade, rather than modelling such trade explicitly;
- the lack of any dynamic interaction between trade and growth;

- the modelling of non-tariff barriers in terms of their *ad valorem* tariff equivalents, when it was evident from economic theory that the equivalence broke down in all but the most simple situations; and
- the increasing importance of such protective devices as anti-dumping actions.

Later generations of trade models have attempted to meet the final four criticisms, although rarely simultaneously. The basic modelling approach has however remained the same. At the same time, the focus of attention has tended to shift to specific issues rather than global concerns.

Imperfect competition, international trade and integration

Some studies of the effects of regional trade arrangements have been conducted within the constant-returns-to-scale/perfectly-competitive-markets framework used in the modelling of international trade. Intra-industry trade is then modelled using the Armington assumption. The Miller and Spencer (1977) analysis of the consequences of the UK entering the EC suggested a small terms of trade gain for the UK that would be outweighed by its budgetary contribution. The Harrison *et al.* (1989) analysis of the EC suggested that all member countries would lose if they left the EC, but that the losses would in general be small. The Hamilton and Whalley (1985) examination of the consequences of the US forming a free trading bloc with various groups of other countries again suggested that the welfare effects would not be large. A more detailed description of the structures and results of these models is given in Table 3.6.

One of the most actively pursued developments has been the modelling of different market structures, and the study of the effects of trade policy within such a framework. Among the earliest and most influential work is that of Harris (1984) and Harris and Cox (1984) on Canadian trade policy. This work continued the Canadian tradition of examining the interaction of trade policy and market structure (see for example Eastman and Stykolt (1960, 1967)), which had suggested that the effect of Canadian tariff policy had been to encourage collusion between a small number of domestic firms and to foster production inefficiencies.

TABLE 3.6 COMPETITIVE COUNTERFACTUAL ANALYSES OF REGIONAL TRADE ARRANGEMENTS (No Market Structure/Scale Economies)

Study	Approach	Regional Scenarios	Main Conclusions
Miller & Spencer (1977)	Static general equilibrium. Armington structure with 2 final goods per country. Constant returns to scale and perfect competition.	2 scenarios for the UK joining the EC, involving the abolition of mutual tariffs and the imposition of the EC common tariff. First involves the UK transferring 90% of its tariff revenue to the EC, while the second does not.	UK gains from a small terms of trade gain. This is more than offset by the transfer to the European budget. Price of agricultural goods rises by 22% compared to manufactured goods. Under the no-transfer scenario, UK increases its manufactured trade with the EC by 50%. UK increases its agricultural imports from the EC by 72% and decreased its imports from the Commonwealth by 0.8%.
Hamilton & Whalley (1985)	Static general equilibrium model, with 8 world blocs and 6 goods per country, 5 of which are tradable. Armington assumption used. Constant returns to scale and perfect competition.	FTAs between the US and each of the other 7 blocs. 3 FTAs involving EC and Japan, the Industrial Countries and the NICs and the LDCs. Intensive examination of an FTA between the US and EC.	Developed countries always gain from an FTA with the US, NICs and the LDCs lose. Only the FTA of the US and the EC is examined in detail with US exports rising by 9.7% to the EC, and EC exports rising by 5.8% to the US. US exports less to, and imports more from, other areas. Reverse is true for the EC.
Harrison, Rutherford & Wooton (1989a)	Static general equilibrium model. 11 regions and 6 goods, all tradable. Armington assumption used. Constant returns to scale and perfect competition. Non-tariff barriers (as well as tariffs, etc.) of 40% between non-EC countries and 20% between EC members.	Eight cases of various countries leaving the EC (with CAP remaining in place). Eight cases of each country leaving the EC (non CAP)	All EC countries have welfare reductions on leaving. US has a small welfare gain. Highest loss is for Ireland (8% of GDP). Smallest losses occur for France and Italy (0.9% of GDP).

Source: adapted from Srinavasan, Whalley and Wooton (1993)

The Harris model specified decreasing average costs for individual firms, with each firm facing fixed (rather than sunk) costs. Harris then analysed the effects of various unilateral and multilateral liberalisation policies within a series of different market structures and assumed pricing rules. The market structure variants included collusive behaviour around the world price gross of the tariff as well as traditional imperfect competition. The most striking consequence of this analysis was the conclusion that the gains to Canada from either bilateral or multilateral trade liberalisation could be as high as 8 - 10 per cent of GNP, considerably greater than would be suggested by a traditional competitive model. The reduction in collusive behaviour appears to be the most important source of this increase in the gains from liberalisation, although in all cases gains come from the reduction in the number of domestic firms and the consequent increase in the output of each remaining firm.

The rate of development in the modelling of imperfectly competitive behaviour since the Harris work has been relatively slow. This may in part reflect recent developments in the literature on the role of market structure in international trade, which has shown that many of the theoretical results are strongly dependent on the assumptions made. For example, the original Brander and Spencer argument that profits may be shifted between countries by the use of an export subsidy requires that Cournot behaviour be assumed; if Bertrand conjectures are used then the required policy for profit shifting is an export tax. Nevertheless, the incorporation of market structure issues has been attempted by other CGE modellers, often as a modification of an existing Heckscher-Ohlin form of model. This trend has been particularly marked in analyses of the effects of regional integration, particularly of the EC and the formation of the North American Free Trade Area. So, for example, Brown and Stern (1989) modified an earlier Deardorff and Stern (1986) model in order to examine the effects of market structure within the Canada-U.S. free trade area negotiations, and found that their results differed substantially according to the structural assumptions made. This work has been continued in the Brown, Stern and Deardorff (1992) model This model is structurally very similar to the Brown and Stern (1989) model (like others, a variant of the 'Michigan model'). The three NAFTA countries (US, Canada, Mexico) are modelled individually, with the remainder of the world modelled as two blocs, one a composite of 31 major trading nations, the other the rest of the world (determined as a residual). The model considers 29 commodities of which 6 are non-tradables. Sectors are modelled as either perfectly competitive or monopolistically competitive with free entry/exit. Perfectly competitive sectors are assumed to employ variable amounts of capital, labour and intermediate products, and to set price equal to marginal cost. The monopolistically competitive sectors need, in addition, fixed amounts of capital and labour, and maximise profits by charging the optimal mark-up. The base year is 1989 for production, employment and trade, but input-output coefficients are taken from data for 1977 in the US, 1976 in Canada and 1980 in Mexico. There is a single representative consumer in each country; each having preferences that are represented by a 2-level nested function (CES inside Cobb-Douglas).

Brown *et al.* conducted five experiments:

- a full NAFTA;
- a full NAFTA plus liberalisation of capital import restrictions by Mexico;
- bilateral tariff elimination by the US and Mexico alone;
- bilateral tariff elimination by US and Mexico alone plus liberalisation of capital import restrictions by Mexico;
- bilateral tariff elimination by US and Canada alone.

They concluded that all potential NAFTA members would gain under each scenario - the US by 0.1% to 0.3 % of GDP, Canada by 0 to 0.7%, Mexico by 0 to 5.0%. The US would always gain on its terms of trade (by between 0.1 and 0.2%), but Canada and Mexico never enjoy such gains (the losses are between 0.1 and 0.0% for Canada, 2.5 to 0.0% for Mexico). The US would also always gain in terms of both the real wage and the real rental on capital. Canada might lose, but would be more likely to make a modest gain. Mexico might also lose but would be more likely to make a substantial gain (up to 9.3%). The simulations also suggested that under each liberalisation scenario there would be an increase in the output per firm in every sector in the US and Canada as a consequence of rationalisation. Intra-industry trade increases under all scenarios, and there is also. an increase in inter-sectoral specialisation, especially in Mexico. Trade between the NAFTA members and the 'other 31 major trading nations' was generally predicted to decrease.

Mercenier (1992) has constructed a model for the analysis of the formation of the Single European market that also embodies non-competitive sectors. The model consists of 6 'countries', Britain, Germany, France, Italy, the 'Rest of EC', and the

'Rest of OECD'. There are 9 sectors - 4 of which are perfectly competitive, and 5 non-competitive, with increasing returns to scale and differentiated products. Various alternative market structures and factor mobility assumptions are used: Cournot and Bertrand conjectures, with and without free entry, and with and without factor mobility within the Single Market. There is a single representative consumer in each country, and the Armington assumption is employed. The base year for calibration of the model is 1982. The model's assumptions were designed to follow those made in Smith and Venables partial equilibrium approach. The results of Mercenier's simulations suggest that in all cases there would be a significant fall in prices in the non-competitive sectors, accompanied by an increase in wages and capital rentals. There would be significant re-allocation effects between sectors, but the overall consequences for welfare would be modest. Table 3.7 summarises the structures and the results of the imperfectly-competitive/scale-economies regional integration models that have been discussed above, and also of some others.

TABLE 3.7 IMPERFECTLY COMPETITIVE COUNTERFACTUAL ANALYSES OF REGIONAL TRADE ARRANGEMENTS (With Market Structure/Scale Economies)

Study	Approach	Regional Scenarios	Main Conclusions
Harris & Cox (1984) and Harris (1984)	Static GE model. Assumes 9 CRS perfectly competitive industries and 20 IRS non-competitive industries. IRS firms have constant per unit variable costs as well as fixed costs. Canada takes import prices as given, but can affect export prices. Armington assumption is used. Representative agent who maximises utility.	Unilateral Free Trade (UFT) where Canada sets all of its tariffs to zero. Multilateral Free Trade (MFT) where Canada and the rest of the world set their tariffs to zero. Selective tariff cuts in 12 of the 20 IRS industries. Bilateral Free Trade (BFT) with the US. Sectoral Free Trade (SFT) with the US in textiles, steel, agricultural machinery, urban transport equipment and chemicals.	Canada receives welfare gains of 4%, 8.6%, 9% and 1.5% of GDP under scenarios UFT, MFT, BFT and SFT. Canada's trade volumes with the world increase by 55%, 90%, 88.2% and 14.5% with UFT, MFT, BFT and SFT. Canada's trade volume increases by 98.7% and 13.6% with the US under BFT and SFT. Real wages in Canada rise by 9.5%, 25%, 28% and 5.7% under UFT, MFT, BFT and SFT.

TABLE 3.7: continued

Baldwin (1992)	Small dynamic model of gains from trade for the EC. Single infinitely lived consumer and IRS technology. Discount rate, inter-temporal elasticity of substitution and capital share of income are 0.05, 0.1 and 0.3. Divergence of social and private returns on capital due to IRS.	Integration of EC markets assumed to lower non-tariff trade barriers. Static gains calculated by Cecchini *et al.* (1988) are dynamised.	Dynamic welfare effects from trade liberalisation increases welfare from between 15% and 90% of the static gains.
Mercenier (1992)	Partial and general equilibrium analyses to study the integration of segmented EC markets in 1992. 4 CRS and 5 IRS sectors. Armington assumption for the CRS sectors. Single representative consumer. Capital and labour only domestically mobile in the short run but capital internationally mobile in the long run.	Bertrand and Cournot conjectures. Sector-by-sector integration. Complete EC integration. The short run fixes the number of firms while the long run allows the number of firms to vary.	For partial integration, there are small welfare increases for EC countries, mixed results for the Rest of OECD. Output rises and number of firms and average costs of firms fall. No trade effects reported. For complete integration, there are also small welfare gains for the EC countries with the Rest of OECD experiencing virtually no change. Terms of trade generally increase for all of the EC countries and fall for the Rest of the OECD. No trade effects reported.
Smith, Venables & Gasiorek (1992)	General equilibrium study of gains from lowering non-tariff trade barriers and the integration of segmented markets in the EC. 14 IRS and 1 CRS sectors. Factors of production include 4 types of labour, capital and intermediate goods. Single representative consumer. For each country and industry, firms are symmetric.	Markets either segmented or integrated. Cournot conjectures. Short run with a fixed number of firm, long run with a variable number of firms.	Welfare increases from 0.2% of GDP for Germany in short run, to 1.4% for EC South in long run under segmented markets. For integrated markets, the range is 0.23% increase for Germany in short run, to 2.9% for EC South in long run. Under segmented markets, changes in exports by EC to ROW range from a decrease of 0.38% in banking and finance in short run, to 8.3% increase in transport equipment in long run. Import decreases range from -0.77% for banking and finance in long run, to -20.2% for transport equipment in long run. Under integrated markets, the absolute value of these effects are approximately doubled.

Source: adapted from Srinavasan, Whalley and Wooton (1992)

Other applications

Other attempts to follow the Harris approach, albeit in modified form, are the modifications of the Whalley (1985) model by Wigle (1988) and Wigle and Nguyen (1989), and the IMPACT model of Dixon *et al.*.

As noted above, the theoretical literature has demonstrated that the conventional practice of modelling policy instruments in terms of their *ad valorem* equivalents may be ill-advised. Many instruments do not fit satisfactorily into the tariff-equivalent framework, and in some cases the approach can even lead to endogenous variables changing in the wrong direction. There have been accordingly considerable efforts to improve the modelling of non-tariff instruments. The Whalley and Wigle (1988) study of the proposed liberalisation of agricultural trade in the Uruguay Round showed that modelling U.S. wheat policy in an *ad valorem* equivalent framework would be highly misleading. Price supports to U.S. farmers are conditional on their agreement to participate in the Set-Aside Programme, and not all farmers have found that it pays to participate. If the price support system is modelled as a production subsidy then the effect of increasing price support must mimic the effects of increasing that subsidy, and must therefore lead to an increase in output and so either in exports or in stocks. Whalley and Wigle however allow for the possibility that an increase in the level of price support, while increasing output per acre, may bring more farmers into the Set Aside Programme, in which case the amount of land set aside will also increase. It follows that the effects of higher price support on output will depend on the relative strengths of the two effects. The Whalley and Wigle simulations suggested that the net effect of U.S. wheat support policy in the 1980s had been to depress output, whereas the conventional *ad valorem* analyses had suggested the opposite effect.

Similar divergences between the consequences suggested by *ad valorem* equivalent and more detailed modelling of policies have been found when considering the consequences of voluntary export restraints. Models of this type are more focused than the general global models considered so far, the modellers choosing to construct a 'one-off' model that trades off a simpler structure in favour of a more detailed modelling of particular policies in the sector of interest. Examples of this approach are the de Melo and Tarr (1988) and Tarr (1989) analyses of VERs, which have explicitly modelled the transfer of quota rents to participating export countries, and the Trela and Whalley study of the Multi Fibre Arrangement (MFA). The latter is concerned with the question of whether the participating developing countries gain or lose from the MFA. The modellers chose to model large numbers of consuming and producing countries and of varieties of textile and clothing products, but closed the model by assuming only one other good (residual GDP). The Trela and Whalley (1990) model specifies 38 'countries', the three major developed importing countries (US, EC, and Canada), 34 developing country exporters, and the 'rest of the world'. Textiles and clothing are divided into 14 categories, but the remainder of goods are aggregated into one category. Production possibility frontiers are 'nested CET'. There is a single representative consumer in each country, modelled as having nested CES preferences. The model assumes that textile trade between the developed countries is quota (but not tariff free). Notably, the Armington assumption is not used, the authors arguing that there is little cross-hauling of textiles between the three developed countries modelled and the developing country exporters. The general conclusions of the simulations are that the elimination of the MFA would give a global gain of some $23 billion, of which the US gets $12.3 billion, the EC $2.2 billion, and Canada $0.8 billion, with the developing country exporters as a group gaining $8 billion. The authors conclude that the majority of the developing country exporters would gain if MFA restrictions were abolished.

It has been argued that the failure of CGE models built before 1984 to take adequate account of dynamics limited their use in policy analysis. This shortcoming reflects the general failure of traditional trade theory to develop its handling of dynamic issues. This in turn is a consequence of the interests of policy makers, who are generally concerned with the inter-commodity and inter-country effects of trade policies rather than with the inter-temporal allocation effects of, for example, the investment incentives in different national tax systems. A recent attempt to incorporate dynamic effects into a trade model is that of Goulder and Eichenberg (1989), who seek to analyse the effect of changes in VERs on the U.S. economy. They model the U.S. economy as having 10 sectors, and allow for asset markets and for inter-country flows of investment as well as goods. Both domestic and foreign households are assumed to be forward-looking utility maximisers, making simultaneous consumption and asset-holding decisions, and adjusting portfolios in response to changes in relative rates of return. Current and capital account transactions are modelled explicitly, and balance of payments equilibrium is achieved through changes in exchange rates and rates of return. Their conclusion is that the effects of changes in VERs are much larger than would be suggested by conventional static models, suggesting that models that ignore dynamic effects may be misleading.

Another attempt to incorporate dynamics into a CGE trade model is by Haaland, Norman, Rutherford and Wergeland (1988). Their model is unusual in two respects: it is a (neo-classical) dynamic growth model, and it deliberately mixes partial and general equilibrium approaches. Production, consumption and trade decisions in each sector are modelled in a partial equilibrium framework, but comparative advantage is modelled in general equilibrium terms "at a level of aggregation which is consistent with an interpretation of comparative advantage in terms of broadly defined activities". The model assumes putty-clay technology, rational expectations on the part of investors, but a constant savings rate. The authors admit to an inconsistency in the differences in modelling investment and savings, but justify it on the grounds of the major increase in model dimensions that would result if savers also were assumed to have perfect foresight. The model specifies six regions (Western Europe, North America, Japan, the OPEC countries, the newly industrialised countries and the non-oil-exporting developing countries). Labour is categorised as either skilled or unskilled. Capital also takes two forms - old and sector specific, and new and sectorally mobile . There is one non-tradable good, two tradable inputs (oil and 'others'), three tradable final goods (one of each intensive in capital, labour and skilled labour). Oil goes to final demand as well as being an intermediate input. Production is specified in terms of a 2-level CES. Consumption is specified as CES. The model is calibrated to a 1979 benchmark.

The most striking conclusion from their simulation runs is that, for a range of scenarios, they repeatedly obtained counterintuitive results for Western Europe. More detailed analysis suggested that Western Europe is essentially a "swing producer" in that changes in her comparative advantage are best understood as a reflection of the changes in the pattern of comparative advantage in the other regions.

3.4 Summary and Conclusions

Policy-relevant implications from CGE modelling

Tax incidence and tax reform

- CGE models have suggested that tax and subsidy systems may reduce welfare substantially compared with the predictions of the standard Harberger-type model.
- In contrast with incidence calculations, CGE analyses have suggested that tax systems do have a major redistributive effect.
- The introduction of risk and financial modelling may reverse the sign of change in some cases compared with the standard Harberger-type model.
- The marginal cost of increasing tax revenue may be substantial.
- Intertemporal and inter-asset distortions are important.

Environmental models

- Carbon taxes reduce global welfare and global GDP.
- Different instruments may result in substantial differences across regions in the cost of reducing carbon usage.
- The economic costs of a carbon tax are lower than those of a general energy tax or a general *ad valorem* tax.

Trade and Integration Studies

- Gains from GATT-based liberalisation are distributed unevenly among members.
- A 'comprehensive' outcome to the Uruguay Round would yield substantially greater gains than would an outcome concentrated on tariff reductions.
- The effects of trade policy are considerably larger when imperfectly competitive behaviour is modelled explicitly.
- Existing levels of protection may be below those that would maximise national welfare.
- Gains from both liberalisation and regional integration are substantially increased via pro-competitive effects if there are imperfectly competitive markets.

Qualifications to the use of CGE modelling

Tax incidence and tax reform

- The formulation of a tax adopted for the purposes of modelling may have an important effect on the outcome.
- There are uncertainties in the literature about appropriate elasticity values, especially for labour supply and savings.
- The functional forms usually employed (CES, LES) are restrictive, but the available alternatives do not behave well for large changes.
- Closure of the model, as in the treatment of foreign trade, of investment and savings, and of government expenditures etc. may have an important effect on the outcome.

Environmental models

- Forward-looking behaviour is not always well represented.
- The long time horizon (necessarily) adopted, and the associated assumptions made about technical progress, adjustment and expectations are very important in determining model outcomes, especially the formulation of 'back-stop' technologies.
- Estimates of elasticity of substitution between energy and non-energy inputs vary widely.

Trade and Integration Studies

- The use of the Armington assumption may lead to greater terms of trade effects from policy changes than is reasonable.
- There are difficulties in modelling some policy instruments (such as quotas and VERs), which will affect model outcomes.
- There is a general failure to model dynamics explicitly, which may lead to the understatement of the gains from trade liberalisation.

Chapter 4. Evaluation of the Methodology

Having reviewed the principles and practice of CGE modelling, we are now in a position to evaluate its usefulness as an input to the policy appraisal process. We do so by assessing the perceived strengths and weaknesses of the approach, followed by an evaluation of the value added it gives in comparison with alternative approaches to modelling. For expositional reasons we will focus on strengths and weaknesses in isolation, and will balance the two in the overall assessment. This is particularly useful in that it allows us to comment on strategies for dealing with perceived weaknesses. Strengths are summarised in Table 4.1, weaknesses in Table 4 .2. In both tables we list these in order of importance (though in the text we discuss them by reference to the stages of analysis).

4.1 Strengths

From the discussion in Chapters 1, 2 and 3, it should be apparent that a key strength which CGE modelling enjoys over most alternatives lies in its solid microfoundations. In constructing a model, the modeller has to lay bare the sub-structure of the economy. Unlike many alternatives, the behaviour of consumers, producers and the government is then explicitly modelled. The role which alternative behavioural assumptions play in determining model outcomes is transparent. This is one of the key strengths of CGE analysis. Clearly, from the standpoint of assessing policy changes at the micro level this is extremely valuable. This transparency also means that should the model generate a solution that seems 'counter-intuitive' then it is possible to determine the probable cause(s) of that outcome.

The formal structure of a CGE model allows investigation of the consequences of using various functional forms (e.g. for production functions and utility functions). However, the very complexity of large CGE models precludes exhaustive investigations. To examine the effects of a change in the form of one function within a CGE model requires that the model be recalibrated and then run again. To perform a full examination of the effects of two alternate forms for each function in a model with n functions would require running the model $n!$ times. While such an exhaustive investigation may well be considered unnecessary, and in many cases it may be sufficient to conduct just a few such tests, it is nevertheless the case that investigating the effects of a set of changes in the assumed structure of a model can be very difficult. Note that so far we have considered just the possibility of changing the functional form. When we take into account the fact that many parameters are specified by the modeller (such as the substitution parameter in a CES function), then it is evident that a full sensitivity analysis is infeasible.

To be more specific, the demand side of a CGE model is typically fairly simple. In many instances it is assumed that there is just one 'representative' consumer; even where different groups are specified, the number is rarely large. An analysis of the effects of changing the specification of preference functions (say from CES to LES) may not be too time-consuming. Similarly, examination of the effects of changing the elasticity of substitution between imports and domestically produced goods is straightforward. On the other hand, a sensitivity analysis of the production structure of the economy, which typically has many sectors, will be much more laborious.

TABLE 4.1 CHECKLIST OF STRENGTHS OF THE CGE APPROACH

- Benefits of Having Solid Microfoundations
- Ability to Include Explicit Welfare Effects
- Distributional Aspects
- Facility for Evaluating Second Best Situations
- Capacity for Disaggregation to Sub-Structure
- Ability to Model Non-Marginal Changes
- Coherent Structure for Evaluating 'Complex' Problems
- Facility for Simulation of Alternatives
- Framework for Evaluating Interdependencies and Feedbacks
- Ability to Model Instrument Constraints
- Confronts Modeller with 'The Problem'.

The process of constructing a CGE model will give some assistance in identifying those functions and assumptions that should be investigated, since the modeller will have some 'feel' for the robustness of the judgements made at various points. Nevertheless, some general guidelines may be offered on those that should be considered. These are assumptions about: (a) the market structure (e.g. whether perfectly or imperfectly competitive); (b) the structure of government taxation and disbursements (between production sectors and between consumer groups); (c) the closure specified by the model.

A good example of the importance of functional forms and behavioural assumptions, and of the problems involved in investigating their effects of changes, is provided by the Cox and Harris (1984) analysis of the gains from a Canadian-U.S. free trade area. Their model, which suggested welfare gains considerably in excess of those previously obtained, departed from the 'standard' perfect-competition/constant-returns-to-scale format in several ways. The Cox and Harris estimates reflect the assumptions made, particularly in not explicitly modelling sunk costs.

An illustration of the importance of the role played by assumptions on the nature of government involvement in the economy, and of the ability of CGE models to produce results which are 'counter-intuitive' but nevertheless correct, is given by the Borges, Goulder and Shoven (1985) study of a windfall profits tax in the US. The profits accrued to owners of energy resources as world prices increased, and intuition might suggest that such a tax would be progressive. The model suggested that the tax might in fact be regressive. This outcome follows from the assumption that the government would disburse the additional revenue in the same proportions as before. Since US government expenditures tend to be on capital-intensive goods, increased expenditure will in practice increase the demand for, and raise the price of, capital and so will be regressive.

The effort required to conduct a sensitivity analysis of a complex CGE model is a necessary price to be paid for the gains that may be made. Such a model gives us a framework for analysing numerically issues which could not be handled by less sophisticated approaches. There are six dimensions to this: the scale of the model, the attention that such models focus on interdependences, the ability to 'enrich' the model by disaggregating sectors of interest, the freedom both to evaluate non-marginal policy changes, and to consider a wide range of policy options within a common framework, and the attention that is necessarily given to the efficiency gains and losses of different policies and their distributional effects.

It will be apparent from the preceding discussion, that we are not confined to working in small dimensions. The scale of a CGE model is eventually determined by data availability, the capacity of the software and hardware, and the time available to the modeller. As we saw in Chapter 2 there is of course a trade off between model scale and complexity - larger models are computationally more difficult to solve and may require more by way of parameterisation/calibration. In principle however, we can build them with large dimensions. Good illustrative examples are the large multi-country trade models and the larger of the carbon tax models discussed in Chapter 3.

The very essence of general equilibrium is that 'everything depends on everything else'. Interdependences and feedbacks, between policy instruments as well as sectors, have an important impact on outcomes, but in practise are difficult to model in anything other than a general equilibrium framework. Clearly, any approach which is partial equilibrium in flavour faces the 'other things being equal' constraint. The CGE approach not only exposes interdependences, it offers a facility for modelling them, if necessary in alternative ways. Closely related to this is the ability to bring instrument constraints into play more readily. This clearly gives the analyst greater flexibility, especially when evaluating the impact of alternative policy reform packages.

The degree to which particular sectors are aggregated will, as we have argued before, depend to a large extent on the purposes for which the model is constructed. Should a particular aggregated sector prove to be of interest however then, subject to data constraints, it is a relatively straightforward task to disaggregate it. It may of course be the case that the model being used is based on a larger model, in which case all that is required is to modify the aggregation procedure that has been used.

Another important dimension is that CGE models can be used to evaluate non-marginal changes. This is in marked contrast to the familiar analysis of the general equilibrium effects of policy changes using differential calculus. (Although, as noted earlier, non-marginal changes may be approximated by a series of smaller changes - the essence of the Johansen approach.) Since many (proposed) policy changes are non-marginal - such as the introduction of a carbon tax, or the abandonment of voluntary export restraints - this offers a considerable gain.

Since CGE modelling is directed at evaluating the response of the economy, and agents therein, to alternative policy shocks, it is an approach that facilitates simulation of alternatives. This of course is also an attribute of macroeconometric models, but the CGE approach offers two advantages over such models. The first, which we deal with next, is that macroeconometric models are designed to 'explain' the pattern of economic activity in the economy as a whole, or some sub-sector(s) thereof. The second is that it is relatively difficult to incorporate certain policy measures within the macroeconomic framework.

The most distinctive and most important attribute of CGE modelling is that it gives us the ability to assess the impact of policy changes on both 'efficiency' and on 'equity'. Economic theory provides us with the tools to rank policy instruments on efficiency grounds, and gives us guidance on their likely distributional aspects. There are however instances where an *a priori* ranking is not possible, and others where the available theories are based on a limited range of economic structures. CGE allows us to model alternative structures and to compare outcomes numerically. As we saw earlier, this is helpful to policy appraisal on a wide range of problems.

What much of this adds up to is the point that CGE models facilitate the ranking of second best changes. Much theoretical discussion of policy intervention is blighted by the nihilism of second best theory. By imposing the constraint that the benchmark data set represents some kind of general equilibrium, a range of deviations from that situation can be explored. Of course, as we shall see in the next section, an obvious objection is that the initial representation of general equilibrium may be highly misleading, particularly where markets are imperfectly competitive. So long as we can regard it as "reasonable" in some sense however, we have a framework for assessing second best situations.

Generally, CGE models attempt to model welfare changes explicitly through the use of indicators such as compensating and equivalent variation. Thus, rather than just identifying the price or quantity effects of a given policy shock we can use the framework to identify the net welfare benefits of alternative strategies/scenarios using a measure of welfare which has firm theoretical foundations. In the context of providing advice on policy, this is an invaluable attribute.

Related to this, since most CGE models are built up from explicit models of the sub-structure, we can assess the impact of policy changes on particular sub-sectors. Since all policy changes have distributional consequences - whether deliberate or unintentional - the ability to identify and compute distributional changes at the micro level is an attractive feature of this approach. Not only is the information interesting in its own right, it may be helpful in informing discussions about appropriate adjustment assistance. From the standpoint of appraising policy, this is probably the most distinctive and valuable feature of CGE modelling. Assessment of welfare and distributional consequences is beyond the scope of many modelling strategies, yet is clearly central to policy appraisal. As we saw in assessing the output of tax and environmental models, many of the really interesting issues are distributional. CGE is almost unique in offering a coherent framework for addressing these.

4.2 Weaknesses

Our discussion in Chapters 2 and 3 revealed a number of potential weaknesses with this approach. One strength which we noted was the explicit microfoundations upon which CGE models are constructed. In principle these models can accommodate any functional form. In practice the solution methods and parameterisation considerations constrain modellers to work with a small number of relatively straightforward/tractable functional forms. Of course, if the world is CES or Cobb-Douglas (or if agents' behaviour is consistent with these) then that does not matter. But, we do not know. Moreover, we do not have any facility for testing the appropriateness of particular functional forms, and indeed model structures more generally, within the CGE model. We cannot compare actual and fitted values, or apply a battery of diagnostic test statistics as a basis for deciding how well a particular model 'fits' and what degree of confidence we should have in its output. Alternatives such as macroeconomic modelling do have the facility for diagnostic testing (although as we shall see later this has its own shortcomings). On the other hand, there is a substantial body of microeconomic literature on the fitting of various functional forms to production and consumption data, and the functional forms most often assumed by CGE modellers reflect the overall judgement that such functions as CES, LES etc. perform well in such econometric studies.

TABLE 4.2 CHECKLIST OF WEAKNESSES OF THE CGE APPROACH

- Simplicity of Functional Forms
- Sensitivity to Closure Rules
- Inter-temporal Substitution and Dynamics
- Inability to 'Test' Model Structure
- Parameterisation and Calibration
- Derivation of Benchmark Data Set
- Equilibrium' Characteristic of Benchmark Scenario
- Expectations
- Primitive Monetary Sectors
- Uniqueness of Solution

Parameterisation and calibration of the chosen functional forms are related problems. As we saw earlier, many of the parameters in the benchmark data sets are point estimates from secondary sources, or are based on the modeller's judgement. This is especially common in respect of elasticities. Often the resulting estimates are drawn from different time periods, or different countries than the time period/country to which the model pertains. Then, to get the model to reproduce the benchmark data set, some parameters need to be calibrated. The justification for the values which emerge from the calibration process is that they are consistent with the benchmark data set, and that since that reproduces a state where the economy is in equilibrium, the values are defensible. Equilibrium is an heroic assumption and as noted earlier we have no means of checking on the validity of calibrated values.

Two other structural features of CGE models are potential weaknesses - the uniqueness of particular solution values, and the closure rules which are used. The former is essentially a technical issue - the modelling framework presumes a unique equilibrium, and delivers solution values on that basis. In principle there could be multiple equilibria. However, there is no reported case of multiple equilibria, and it may be argued that the 'well-behaved' nature of the functional forms usually employed makes it unlikely that they would exist. Certainly, the one extensive search for multiple equilibria that has been reported in the literature failed to find more than one solution.

Closure is more serious. This is often effected via the imposition of a balanced budget, or balanced trade, or a savings-investment identity. Not only are results typically sensitive to the closure rule adopted, its choice can constrain the model in important respects. If for example we close via a savings-investment identity and treat 'savings' as if it were just another bundle of consumer goods (as some models do), we get a passive investment function. This raises a further weakness: intertemporal flows are typically not well handled in these models. This does not only apply to savings-investment decisions, but also to growth processes more generally. If the model is being used for simulation purposes, this is a serious shortcoming, (well illustrated in fact in the context of 'green models'). Expectations are generally either ignored, or modelled mechanistically. Depending on the nature of the problem being addressed this too can be a serious deficiency.

Finally we should note that in most CGE models monetary sectors are generally quite primitive, and monetary flows are ignored. One defence for this is that the models are concerned with relative prices and as such are only concerned with real variables. Not everyone would find that wholly convincing.

4.3 Value Added *vis-à-vis* Alternative Approaches

The other approaches to policy modelling and appraisal with which we shall compare CGE modelling may be divided into four main groups, summarised in Table 4.3.

For the purposes of this monograph we shall ignore the time series approach. Time series models have an important role to play in providing a benchmark against which the forecasting ability of macro- and microeconometric models may be judged. They may also give important insights into the lag structures that should be used in such models, and may be used to give predictions of the values of variables in the absence of a policy change. They have in general however little direct basis in economic theory, and rarely attempt to offer any insight into the structure of the economy or the effects of policy variables. In particular there is no possibility of using such a model *per se* as an *ex ante* guide to the effects of a policy change.

TABLE 4.3 ALTERNATIVES TO CGE MODELLING

- Those that seek to model the economy in its entirety. These comprise:
  - Formal macroeconometric modelling (the construction and estimation of multi-equation structural models based on economic theory).
  - Time series models of macroeconomic variables (dealing with a small set of equations, perhaps the reduced form of a simple structural model, but paying particular attention to the lag structures of both explanatory variables and disturbance terms).
  - Optimal control models of macroeconomic policy.[11]
- Other economy-wide but 'fix-price' general equilibrium approaches:
  - Input-output and social accounting matrix models.
  - Linear/non-linear comparative static models .
- Other micro-economic approaches founded in partial equilibrium analysis:
  - Formal applied partial equilibrium models.
  - Time series models of microeconomic variables.
  - Dynamic programming models/dynamic optimisation/optimal control models.
- Intuition, based on either partial equilibrium analysis or relatively simple general equilibrium models.

We shall pay as little attention to the use of intuition based on partial (whether theoretical or applied) and 'simple' general equilibrium models. Although both may give us important insights into the possible consequences of policy changes, and allow us to make a partial (and particular) ranking policies in terms of their desirability, they cannot be taken as serious competitors to CGE modelling. They do of course provide the underpinnings for CGE analysis, and have a role to play in the interpretation and validation of the results of a CGE exercise. However, as we noted earlier in this section, partial equilibrium analysis must, by its very nature, exclude those interdependences which are at the heart of any general equilibrium approach, while simple general equilibrium models suffer from their very simplicity and their inability to provide numerical answers to problems. This then leaves us with the 'fix-price', dynamic optimisation/optimal control (DO/OC), and macroeconometric models.

Fix-price models enjoy a richness of specification of the production sectors of an economy that approaches that of CGE models. They suffer however from a major drawback, in that their structure rules out consideration of the essential element of a market economy - the adjustment of prices to changes in the economy and the consequent adjustment of quantities bought and sold. In particular, they use an extremely simplistic formulation of the demand side of the economy. Fix-price models are best suited to the analysis of a 'command' economy. Nevertheless, there is a close linkage between fix-price and CGE models in that both attempt to model the microeconomic structure of an economy, and both rely on a similar data set.

It is debatable whether either formal macroeconometric or optimal control/dynamic optimisation models should be seen as competitors or as complements to CGE models. They are competitors in that both they and CGE models seek to explain the response, over time, of the economy as a whole to changes in economic policy. In the same sense, the microeconomic DO/OC models compete with CGE models as ways of modelling changes within specified sectors over time. Both however are complements to CGE models in that what may be seen as the weaknesses of one approach may equally be judged to be the strengths of the other. All however share common weaknesses.

Formal macroeconometric models are strong in their ability to deal with dynamic issues, such as expectations, capital accumulation, resource depletion and economic growth, and have a firm base in economic theory. They also have distinct advantages in their ability to encompass monetary variables and market disequilibrium. Finally, they are estimated econometrically, with all that implies in terms of confidence intervals and so on. Computable general equilibrium models lack, for the most part, these attributes, although some attempts have been made to include money variables, and some simple multi-period models have been constructed (as opposed to single period models being linked through simple updating procedures). Certainly it is the case that most CGE models treat investment decisions in a very naive way, reflecting the difficulty of incorporating forward-looking behaviour in such a model.

On the other hand, macroeconometric models generally lack detail on the microeconomic structure of the economy. This has two major consequences. First, the well-documented problems of aggregation suggest that the production, investment and consumption functions upon which macroeconometric models are built may be a poor reflection of the microeconomic structure. Moreover, macroeconometric models take little explicit account of the competitive structure of the economy. Second, they are by and large incapable of providing fine detail on the distributional and efficiency consequences of policy changes. These may both be regarded as strengths of the CGE approach. Although the functional forms assumed for, say, production functions in a typical CGE model are of necessity rather straightforward, and their parameterisation could be much improved, they do allow for a differential treatment of sectors. At the same time such production functions, and the demand functions used in CGE models, are consistent with microeconomic theory.

Macro- and microeconomic DO/OC models have the advantage of being designed to track the movement of the economy, or some part thereof, over time, and of helping the modeller to select optimal time paths of policy changes according to some clearly specified criteria. Macroeconomic DO/OC models however share with the formal macroeconometric models an inability to model distributional and welfare effects. Microeconomic DO/OC models, on the other hand, are almost invariably based on partial equilibrium theorising, and so lack the ability to encompass those interactions and interdependences that are the focus of CGE modelling.

Macroeconometric, DO/OC and CGE models have in common the problems of the adequacy of available data for their purposes, presumptions about structural forms, parameterisation, and the role of the modeller. The dominant data problem for the macroeconometric modeller is the time-consistency of the information he is using. The adequate modelling structure of shifts, particularly when these and their effects are spread out over time, is an unresolved issue. This difficulty is compounded by the inability to model the use of some policies if they have not been used before, and the complete inability to model the use of others. The CGE modeller, on the other hand, must compile data for a 'typical' year (or average of years), and must constrain that data to meet the specifications of a Walrasian model.

All three forms of modelling require that assumptions be made about functional forms. Although the econometric modeller has the facility for testing the adequacy of a given functional form, he is limited by time and the availability of data in the range of forms he can investigate. This is of course particularly so in the case of dynamic structures. The CGE modeller must also of course make assumptions about the functions used in the model, and cannot test the appropriateness of his assumptions, although he can appeal to other work to justify his choice(s).

Macroeconometric modelling also has an apparent edge on CGE modelling in terms of the parameterisation of the model, since the modeller may use time series data and employ estimation techniques whose properties are reasonably well understood. The CGE modeller on the other hand must rely on exogenously determined estimates of some parameters, on his judgement about others, and must then calibrate the rest to be consistent with the benchmark data set. The balance is not however absolutely in the favour of the macroeconometric modeller. Current econometric techniques offer only limited help on the estimation of time changing parameters, while the identification and estimation of dynamic relationships has, since the evolution of co-integration techniques, undergone a process of revision which is not yet completed. In the same vein, the modelling of expectations is far from ideal, with the modeller caught between specifying either an empirically implausible rational expectations structure or devising an *ad hoc* structure of his own, Furthermore, the performance of macroeconometric models in a world where the economic structure is suffering rapid change has been unconvincing.

The dynamic complexity of DO/OC models, whether macro- or microeconomic, and the problems involved in the specification and solution of the models, also tends to push the modeller into relying on exogenously determined parameter estimates.

Finally, all three forms of modelling necessarily involve the judgement, experience and biases of the modeller(s). In each case, these are likely to be reflected in the structure that the modeller imposes. In macroeconometric modelling this may be reflected in a model having a 'Keynesian' or a 'monetarist' structure (or some particular variant within those), or in it being essentially *ad hoc* (in which case it is open to the charge of lacking a firm foundation in macroeconomic theory). In CGE modelling the judgement etc. of the modeller is likely to be reflected in his assumptions about the competitive structure of various sectors of the economy (and the associated production technologies), about such parameters as he cannot derive from exogenous sources, and the way in which he chooses to close the model. It is not clear whether the biases on one side will outweigh those on the other.

The general conclusion must be that the three approaches are best seen as mutual complements. All have important strengths and all have major weaknesses, but fortunately weaknesses in one may be compensated by strengths in the other(s). The drawback to this view is that there seems little prospect at the moment of a formal reconciliation between them. Certainly, the assumptions on which they are based, in particular the different views taken of market clearing, make it difficult to envisage more than an 'informal' linking between the two. If reconciliation is to come in the future then it would have to be through the development of dynamic and econometrically estimated computable general equilibrium models, which would then in effect supplant the macroeconometric and DO/OC approaches.

4.4 Summary and Conclusions

The strengths and weakness of the CGE approach are summarised in Tables 4.1 and 4.2. In essence the strengths reflect:

- The micro-economic foundations of general equilibrium analysis, which give the approach the ability to deal with questions of efficiency and distributional equity, and a framework within which one may model interdependences and feedback, the scope to disaggregate problem areas in order to model the sub-structure, and in particular the ability to derive explicit welfare measures.
- The consequent transparency of the models, which allows the modeller to investigate the causes of any apparently counter-intuitive outcomes within a familiar and generally well-documented economic framework.

- The facility to handle complex non-linear equation systems, which in turn allows the economist to evaluate second-best situations, to model constraints on policy instruments, and to simulate multiple policy changes within a given framework.

The weaknesses in turn reflect the difficulties encountered in parameterising a system of many equations when the parameters must meet the requirements of a Walrasian general equilibrium, the theoretical issues inherent in the Walrasian system, and the mathematical difficulties inherent in solving a system of many non-linear equations. Specifically the weaknesses reflect:

- The difficulties of obtaining a benchmark data set that is consistent with a general equilibrium.
- The need to choose relatively simple functional forms in order to facilitate parameterisation and to reduce, if not avoid, the possibility of multiple solutions.
- The inability to 'test' the model structure, except insofar as outcomes are consistent with prior expectations based on the economic knowledge of the modeller.
- Difficulties in modelling dynamic phenomena, such as expectations and inter-temporal substitution, in integrating a sophisticated monetary sector, and in closing the chosen system against exogenous factors

CGE modelling is an approach that considerably enriches the range of methods available to the policy analyst. Its firm microeconomic foundations make it an important complement to some other approaches and a successful competitor to others. In particular, CGE modelling:

- Complements formal macroeconometric modelling by allowing the analysis of distributional and efficiency issues and by providing a framework for modelling interdependences in the economy.
- Is a competitor to, and should eventually supplant for detailed analyses, both fix-price general equilibrium approaches and other microeconomic methods founded on partial equilibrium analyses.

Chapter 5. CGE Modelling and Policy Appraisal

In any science progress is made by confronting testable hypotheses with data generated by real world processes, or experimental situations. The latter is relatively unimportant in economics, for most purposes we rely upon the former. Data generated by economic activity can be utilised in various ways, depending upon the objective of any investigation, and the modelling strategy of the analyst. The objective of a particular investigation may simply be to test a specific hypothesis (e.g. demand for oil is inversely related to its price), but in general, it is likely that investigation will also be targeted at informing the process of policy formulation and policy appraisal (e.g., just how sensitive is the demand for oil to changes in its price; what does that imply about the optimal tax on oil, and so on).

As we have seen, CGE is one of a menu of modelling strategies available for investigating economic relationships, and the responsiveness of agents to various economic stimuli. Alternative approaches include, *inter alia,* macroeconometric modelling; panel based microeconometric modelling; intuition based partial equilibrium modelling; fixed price input-output/linear programming analysis; experimental/data response analysis; and modelling of growth processes. All of these can inform the policy appraisal process to a greater or lesser degree. Having seen the value added associated with CGE, where exactly does it fit in?

5.1 The Scope of CGE Analysis

As we saw in the previous chapter, CGE modelling has a number of distinctive features. In particular if offers a coherent theoretical framework within which complex problems with interdependencies and feedbacks can be handled. Moreover, once a particular model has been constructed and calibrated it can then be used to evaluate the impact of a menu of policy changes, under a range of different circumstances. The technical sophistication of the CGE approach makes it potentially a very powerful tool for investigation. Clearly this does not mean that all the policy advisor needs in his or her toolbox is an appropriate CGE model. What it implies is that this should be part of a portfolio of instruments available, its use being fashioned by the purpose at hand. When is a CGE approach likely to be most appropriate/most useful?

The answer to this question is determined by several considerations. First, what is the key objective behind a given investigation? Is it to:

- evaluate the impact of a particular policy innovation on a specific sector - for instance the abolition of car tax;
- evaluate the impact of alternative strategies for delivery of a specific public service - for instance the cost effectiveness of methods of screening for colorectal cancer;
- evaluate the distributional consequences of a particular change in a particular sector - for instance the redistributional consequences of the abolition of tax relief on mortgage interest;
- evaluate a policy innovation which is broadly based or narrowly based - for instance, an increase in stamp duty *vis-à-vis* an increase in value added tax;
- evaluate the short-run properties of the economy in response to a given change - for example, the impact on unemployment in 1994 of a tax increase in 1993;
- evaluate the long run properties of the economy in response to a policy innovation - for example, the impact on growth in 2050 of a carbon tax introduced in 1995;
- evaluate the transitional consequences of alternative policy changes - for example the impact on employment of a devaluation *vis-à-vis* an employment subsidy?

Clearly the objective is crucial. In general, if one is interested in small-scale, sector-specific, short-run consequences then it will be inappropriate to build a CGE model - in part because it is unlikely to provide the kind of sharply focused answer required, in part because (notwithstanding the availability of software) these models are relatively expensive to construct. By contrast, if one is interested in the longer run properties of a more broadly based change where distributional effects are likely to be important, then CGE comes into its own. A few examples will serve to make the point.

There would be little point in constructing a CGE model specifically for the purpose of assessing the impact of abolishing car tax. A simple partial equilibrium model, using data on prices, quantities and elasticities would suffice for generating sensible orders of magnitude - even allowing for the fact that there may be income effects associated with such a change, which the partial equilibrium approach would fail to allow for. This does not of course mean that an appropriate CGE model (like the Smith-Venables (1990) model of the car sector), would not offer the facility for additional insights. It would. The point is however that the marginal cost of building a model *specifically* for the purpose of assessing a change in car tax would exceed the marginal benefits of so doing, (and probably to a substantial degree).

Another area where CGE is inappropriate, but for different reasons, is as a device for short-term forecasting. Macroeconometric models which utilise long runs of time series data are far better suited to this purpose. As we have seen, however, when it comes to large scale models where interdependencies and feedbacks are important, and where insights into distributional changes are an objective, CGE most probably represents 'state of the art'. In Chapter 2 we reviewed a number of areas to highlight these strengths - trade and integration studies, environmental models and tax models. In the case of the first of these areas, for some purposes, there are no realistic alternatives to CGE. As an illustration, take the modelling of changes in multilateral trade flows and the impact of a Uruguay Round settlement. The estimates generated by Nguyen, Perroni and Wigle (1990) could not have been derived by any alternative approach. Trade shares analysis can provide some indication of the impact of trade reforms on trade flows, but not much more. Despite the limitations associated with the Nguyen, Perroni, Wigle model, it provides estimates which are an essential ingredient in the policy debate.

'Green models' also offer an agenda where the CGE approach can inform the process of policy appraisal. The scientific uncertainties associated with global warming mean that this is an area where modelling is particularly hazardous, and one can question the utility of estimates of welfare losses associated with given changes over one hundred or two hundred years into the future. Any such estimates are likely to be very sensitive to changes in the structure of the economy and technical change. For these reasons the dynamic programming approach may be a more defensible basis for *forecasting* than CGE. What the latter delivers however is an insight into the potential distributional effects of given changes. This is illustrated well by the Whalley and

Wigle (1990) model. From the standpoint of trying to advance international negotiations, this is the issue which requires further investigation. International negotiations will be influenced more by considerations of the short- to medium-term distributional policy intervention than by long-run forecasts of GDP losses.

As we noted in Chapter 2, one area where the CGE approach has been intensively deployed is in tax analysis. Indeed it is probably more widely used now than the more traditional tax incidence framework. The key feature which again makes it so attractive is the ability to probe distributional effects flowing from changes in tax rates, or the tax base, or systemic reforms. Moreover, since fiscal arrangements are subject to annual reviews, the availability of a model offers the facility for updating, review and recalibration.

This last point raises a second consideration which is germane to the choice of modelling strategy - is the investigation 'one shot' or recurrent? All modelling approaches involve initial set-up costs - CGE, like macroeconometric modelling, involves relatively high (fixed) set-up costs. Clearly, in the context of policy appraisal one should only incur such costs if the model is 're-usable'.

Policy appraisal often involves the evaluation of alternative instruments for achieving a given target, rather than the assessment of a particular intervention. A CGE structure is manifestly superior to alternatives for such counter factual analysis. As before, an example helps to motivate the point. At present the World Bank is investing significant amounts in programme lending. Typically, this takes the form of a commitment on the part of the recipient government to a series of supply side policy reforms. Increasingly appraisal of the potential impact of these reform packages is being assessed in the context of a CGE model. This facilitates the assessment of alternative instrument packages, and helps to make more transparent the consequences of one line of action rather than another.

5.2 Reliance on CGE in Government and International Agencies

It is clear from the previous section that a good case can be made for greater usage of CGE modelling as an input to the policy appraisal process. As with other modelling strategies however, it needs to be utilised in appropriate circumstances. There is little point in constructing a general purpose model designed to satisfy all needs. Two approaches are possible. One could have an in-house specialist facility which can develop, refine and update models as required. Putting in place the hardware and software for this purpose is relatively straightforward, maintaining the required human capital is rather more resource intensive. The alternative approach is simply to commission and maintain a model which is built with a specific need or needs in mind.

Table 5.1 summarises the usage which is presently made of CGE modelling by governmental and by non-governmental agencies. We can see from this table that both approaches have been followed. The OECD and World Bank have a relatively large number of in-house modellers, and a tradition of building and maintaining a range of models. The OECD for example has used the approach to inform their analysis of agricultural reforms, trade reforms and CO_2 emissions abatement. The World Bank. has, for some ten years or so, used the approach as an input to policy appraisal in a large number of developing countries and policy reform scenarios. CGE analyses of the impact of policy reforms in LDCs have now been applied in scores of cases. The technique is used more extensively and more routinely by the World Bank than by any other organisation, (see Greenaway and Milner, 1993). Both the World Bank and OECD appear to have a long-term commitment to the approach. However, both agencies also maintain a portfolio of alternative modelling approaches - most notably macroeconometric model building in the case of OECD and fix-price models in the case of the World Bank.

By contrast agencies like the European Commission and the US Treasury have commissioned work that is problem-specific. In evaluating the potential impact of the EC 1992 programme the Commission used a variety of approaches, one of which was CGE; in assessing the impact of incorporation of the tax system, the US Treasury had a model purpose built. In both of these (and other instances), the model output turned out to be influential. In both cases, it is unlikely that the output could have been generated by an alternative approach. The US government has also invested in model development to inform reforms of agricultural and trade policy.

As we can see from Table 5.1 a large number of other government agencies are consumers of the output of CGE models. The issues addressed are primarily those on which we focused in Chapter 3: tax policy, (e.g. Canada, Mexico, Spain and Italy); environmental policy (e.g. Sweden and Australia); trade and integration (e.g. Canada, Mexico and Germany). The output from these exercises are reported in policy documents and used to underpin policy positions. Most of the exercises involve some blend of outside researchers and in-house capability, where the latter need not involve an explicit ability to run models, but does require a minimum understanding of model structure and interpretative skills to make sensible use of the output. Thus although CGE modelling may not be as common in governmental agencies as microeconometric modelling, it is perceived as having a role to play in policy appraisal, and is becoming increasingly widely used.

5.3. Assessment of the Potential for CGE Analysis in the UK

At present CGE modelling does not have a prominent role to play in government and non-governmental agencies (like the Bank of England) in the UK. In view of the extent to which the approach has been embraced elsewhere, and given the UK's traditional strengths in the areas where CGE is most widely applied (tax analysis and international trade), this is surprising. Why has there been a comparative lack of interest in CGE? is there a case for encouraging further development of the approach? how could any new initiatives be supported?

As we saw in the previous section, the key strength of CGE modelling lies in the ability to handle large-scale models with some account being taken of systemic feedbacks and interdependencies. The menu of problems to which the technique can be applied is as full in the UK as elsewhere. From an analytical and policy standpoint we are just as interested in the consequences of European integration as the Commission; in the distributional consequences of tax reforms as the US Treasury; in the consequences of carbon taxes and so on. Why then have the models not been built? Both demand and supply factors are relevant.

TABLE 5.1 CGE MODELLING AND GOVERNMENT/NON-GOVERNMENTAL AGENCIES

Country/Ministry	Model Focus	Special features
AUSTRALIA		
Industries Assistance Commission - on reference from various ministries	Multiple policy analysis	Flexible multi-purpose capability
BELGIUM		
Various ministries	Price reforms and labour market policies	Unemployment and fixed price equilibria
CANADA		
Ministry of Finance	Trade policy (US-Canada, GATT)	Scale economies/market structure
Ministry of Finance	Tax policy (GST)	Household and commodity detail
MacDonald Commission/ Economic Council of Canada	Regional policies	Interregional migration/trade
GERMANY		
Lander governments	Impacts of EC tax harmonisation	Multiple country analysis of within-EC effects of tax changes
ITALY		
Tax Ministry	Italian tax reform	Tax detail
MEXICO		
Finance Ministry	Tax and trade policies and reforms	Endogenous unemployment
SPAIN		
Finance Ministry	Tax reforms	Detailed commodity/household treatment
SWEDEN		
Environmental and Trade Ministries	Environmental policies - impacts of acid rain	Explicit environmental modelling
UK		
Scottish Office	Scottish agricultural sector	
US		
Office of Tax Analysis, US Treasury	Tax policy	Dynamics, commodity and household detail
Department of Agriculture	Agriculture/Trade	Detail of agriculture programmes
USITC	Trade policy	VERs, other NTBs
OECD		
Economic Studies	Agriculture/GATT	Intercountry effects
	Environment/carbon taxes	Dynamic
	Global trade/GATT Uruguay Round	Multicountry
WORLD BANK		
Regional Operations	Trade, tax, price reform, energy policy, and other areas; multiple models	Focused models on particular country policy issues

Much research, certainly large-scale research, is publicly supported. In general, government agencies have tended to support macroeconometric modelling efforts whether directly (as is the case of the Treasury model), or indirectly (through Research Council and Charitable Foundation support for several programmes). Modelling teams in the UK have therefore tended to cluster around the large macroeconometric modelling efforts. In recent years ESRC has supported the development of Designated Research Centres (DRCs). These however, have tended to be problem-focused rather than techniques-based. The absence of a demand for CGE modelling, and the lack of support for large scale modelling efforts have no doubt contributed to the failure of a modelling centre to emerge in the UK.

As part of our enquiries we surveyed all Economics Departments in the (old) UK universities. Four things are notable from the responses. First, there is quite wide-spread evidence of current activity using CGE techniques in a relatively large number of universities. Indeed, the extent to which an interest is being shown will surprise many. Second there is a relatively wide range of issues being addressed - trade reforms, tax reforms, agricultural reforms and so on. Third, a wide range of software is being used. Some of this is custom-built, some off-the-shelf. Fourth, in almost all cases the initiative depends upon a particular individual. This is a striking, but not altogether unexpected, result.

The extent to which the technique is being adopted reflects, among other things, the proliferation of increasingly user-friendly software in encouraging experimentation with CGE, very often by graduate students. The effort is however diffused and unfocused. There is at present no single 'modelling centre' where an appropriate library of software, hardware and technical support is available for training purposes, and where large scale modelling efforts are underway. These kind of units do exist in North America (for example at the University of Western Ontario, University of Michigan, Stanford University, and World Bank). Not only do these centres provide a focus for research activity with the critical mass of human capital to support large scale, ongoing, model building; they also fulfil the function of a training centre for research students. For example, Western Ontario, Michigan and Stanford Universities have steadily produced a stream of modellers who have moved on to develop resource centres elsewhere. Moreover, such centres also offer the facility for regular interaction between model builders and policy advisors. Again the experiences of Western Ontario, Michigan and Stanford are salutary in this respect. One initiative presently underway, (supported by the World Bank's capacity building programme) is a training initiative targeted at building the human capital base required to support CGE modelling in a number of developing countries.

Should we be encouraging the development of CGE modelling skills in the UK? On the basis of the analysis in Chapters 2 through 5, our answer to this question is yes. There is an obvious menu of policy issues to which the technique can be applied, and the human capital to exploit the techniques most certainly exists. To do so, however, will require a greater concentration of modelling expertise than exists at present. The appropriate mechanisms for securing the investment required are beyond the scope of this report.

5.4 Summary and Conclusions

- CGE offers a coherent theoretical framework for modelling complex interdependencies and feedbacks, and gaining detailed insights into the impact of policy reforms.
- CGE does not provide a template for the analysis of all issues, and it is important to target its use to purposes which take fullest advantage of its strengths. In general, if one is interested in the small-scale, sector-specific, short-run consequences of a policy change, it will be inappropriate to build a CGE model. By contrast, if one is interested in the longer run properties of a more broadly based change where distributional effects are likely to be important, then CGE can be helpful.
- The CGE approach is not well suited to forecasting, which clearly limits its potential. On the other hand however, its facility for counterfactual analysis allows the policy advisor to investigate alternative strategies for hitting a particular target.
- Gives the fixed costs of setting up a CGE facility, models should not be built for 'one-shot' purposes but in a setting where they can be re-applied on a regular basis.
- A large number of governmental, and non-governmental, agencies now make extensive use of the CGE approach. Some have purpose built models, other

collaborate with non-governmental researchers. The models are used to inform a range of issues, including tax environmental and trade policy. The output of many of the models finds its way into official documentation, and is used to underpin policy positions.

- CGE analysis has not figured prominently in the activities of UK governmental agencies, perhaps surprisingly given its usage elsewhere. This is explained partly by the resources which are invested in macroeconometric model building, and partly by the lack of a human capital base to support a serious modelling commitment.
- There is a surprisingly large amount of effort being put into CGE modelling in the UK, although it is in general diffused and unfocused, with initiatives relying heavily on individual researchers. This contrast starkly with the situation in North America where a number of specialist centres, supported by specialist teams exist.
- A strong case can be made for a greater commitment of resources to CGE modelling in the UK.

Notes

1 The bibliography in Appendix D gives details of a number of sources which set out basic principles in some detail. Shoven and Whalley (1992) offer a comprehensive overview.

2 The effects of non-marginal changes in parameters may be approximated by aggregating the effects of successive marginal changes. This is the essence of the Johansen procedure, discussed later.

3 For a discussion of SAMs see Pyatt and Round (1977).

4 Many software packages give the iteration steps as output. It must be remembered that these steps reflect the strategy adopted by the programmer. They must not be taken as an indicator of the adjustment process within the economy being modelled.

5 See Shoven and Whalley (1984), p. 1010. Formally, we could set $P_L = 1$ and solve for the other three prices, the tax revenue, and for the quantity variables X_{11}, X_{21}, K_1, and L_1. The other quantity variables may then be derived from the model.

6 There are various routes that may be used to calibrate model parameters. Consider the parameters ϕ_1, δ_1 and σ_1 of the production function for sector 1 (manufactures). These define the position, slope and curvature of any given isoquant. The benchmark data however only allow us to determine the position and the slope of the isoquant. Recalling that we use the Harberger convention that all prices are set to one in the benchmark equilibrium, we know that 8.532 units of capital and 26.366 units of labour produce 35 units of manufactures. Since both factor prices are equal to 1, we know that the slope of the isoquant at that point is equal to -1. We cannot obtain the curvature directly, so we shall in this case assume a value for the elasticity of substitution, σ_1 (Shoven and Whalley assume a value of 2). Now consider the two factor demand equations specified in the text:

$$L_1 = (1/\phi_1)Q_1\left(\delta_1 + (1-\delta_1)\left(\delta_1 P_K/((1-\delta_1)P_L)\right)^{(1-\sigma_1)}\right)^{\sigma_1/(1-\sigma_1)}$$

$$K_1 = (1/\phi_1)Q_1\left((1-\delta_1) + \delta_1\left((1-\delta_1)P_L/(\delta_1 P_K)\right)^{(1-\sigma_1)}\right)^{\sigma_1/(1-\sigma_1)}$$

Taking the ratio of these and rearranging, remembering that $P_L = P_K = 1$, gives

$$K_1/L_1 = (\delta_1/1-\delta_1)^{\sigma_1}$$

so that we may obtain δ_1 as

$$\delta_1 = \frac{(K_1/L_1)^{1/\sigma_1}}{1+(K_1/L_1)^{1/\sigma_1}}$$

7 See Appendix B.

8 This section draws on the discussion in a survey paper by Whalley (1989) which sets out the more prominent then-available tax models.

9 Such as Pechman and Okner (1974) who suggest that the U.S. tax system does little to redistribute income.

10 But not of all. See for example the Trela *et al.* model of international trade in grains, and the Haaland *et al.* world trade model, in both of which commodities are assumed to be homogeneous.

11 For a survey of the relevance of control theory in policy analysis see Pyndick (1973).

Appendix A: A Glossary of Terms Commonly Used in CGE Modelling

Many of the terms used in CGE analysis are particular to the methodology. In general, terms have been briefly explained when introduced in the text. This appendix gives a full definition and description of the key terms. Those included in the Glossary are as follows:

Allen Elasticities
Armington Assumption
Arrow-Debreu Model
Benchmark Equilibrium Data Set
Brouwer Fixed Point Theorem
Calibration
Constant Elasticity of Substitution (CES) Functions
Constant Elasticity of Transformation (CET)
Closure
Cobb-Douglas Functions
Compensating Variation
Counterfactual Equilibrium
Dynamic General Equilibrium Model
Extended Linear Expenditure System (ELES) Functions
Equivalent Variation
Extraneous Elasticities
Kakutani Fixed Point Theorem
Leontief Functions
Linear Expenditure System Functions (LES)
Merrill's Algorithm
Nesting
Newton's Method
Numéraire
Parameterisation
Policy Appraisal
Pre-selection

R.A.S. Adjustment

Replication Check

Scarf's Algorithm

Simplex

Social Accounting Matrix (SAM)

Two-Sector General Equilibrium Model

Van der Laan and Talman's Algorithm

Allen Elasticities

Cross-elasticities that are widely used in empirical work. They have the attraction of being compensated (i.e. real income is held constant) and symmetric, and typically are share-weighted.

Armington Assumption

An assumption used in trade models whereby domestically produced and imported goods of a similar nature are treated as being qualitatively different. Specifically, products are differentiated according to their origin. This heterogeneity assumption is made mainly to account for the pervasive presence of intra-industry trade which appears in the international trade data to which these models are calibrated.

Arrow-Debreu Model

A theoretical model of Walrasian general equilibrium which is the foundation for applied general equilibrium analysis. Consumers are assumed to have a set of preferences and an initial endowment of a number of commodities. Utility maximisation leads to demand functions for each commodity. Market demands are the sum of each consumer's demand. They depend on all prices, are continuous, non-negative, homogenous of degree zero (no money illusion) and satisfy Walras's Law (at any set of prices, total consumer expenditure equals consumer income). Production technology is described by constant (or non-increasing) returns to scale production functions, and producers maximise profits. Equilibrium is characterised by a set of real prices and levels of production such that market demand equals supply for all commodities. In the constant returns to scale case, this implies that no production activity does better than break even at equilibrium prices.

Benchmark Equilibrium Data Set

An observable data set assumed to represent an equilibrium in the general equilibrium model being considered. This normally requires that the data set be constructed such that market demand equals market supply for each commodity, profits are non-positive in each industry, all domestic agents (including the government) have demands that satisfy their budget constraints and the economy is in external sector balance. As available raw data is typically inconsistent with these requirements, unless it is in the form of a SAM, data modifications and adjustments (such as RAS adjustments) may be necessary to ensure consistency.

Brouwer Fixed Point Theorem

A fixed point theorem concerned with point-to-point mappings of the unit simplex into itself. It is used to demonstrate the existence of a general equilibrium solution (fixed point) in a pure exchange model.

Calibration

A deterministic procedure which computes values for unknown parameters of the functional forms used in an applied general equilibrium model from an observed data set. It is assumed that the data set represents an equilibrium for the general equilibrium model under consideration (benchmark equilibrium data set). The model is then solved for its unknown parameters as functions of the observed data. Typically, calibration uses only one period (or an average over periods) data and a unique solution for all parameter values is not obtained (unless Cobb-Douglas functions are specified throughout). Extraneous estimated values for some parameters, such as elasticities, may be specified, which then permits values of the remaining parameters to be determined uniquely. (See also *parameterisation*).

Constant Elasticity of Substitution (CES) Functions

Demand functions in applied models are often derived assuming CES utility functions. The resulting demand functions are reasonably flexible as they do not enforce unitary own-price elasticity and permit non-zero cross-price elasticities. Unitary income elasticity is assumed, however. On the production side, CES value-added functions are often used to allow for substitution between primary factors.

Constant elasticity of transformation (CET)

A specification for a production possibility curve. If a PPC has this property then a given proportionate change in the relative prices of two commodities results in a constant proportionate change in the product mix.

Closure

A specification made for the behaviour of the external sector in single-country general equilibrium models incorporating trade. Typically, this involves specifying a system of simple export-demand and import-supply functions which the country is assumed to face in its transactions with the rest of the world.

Cobb-Douglas Functions

Demand (production) functions in applied models are sometimes derived assuming Cobb-Douglas utility functions. These demand functions have a very simple structure but are implausibly restrictive, enforcing unitary own-price and income elasticities and zero cross-price elasticities. In this regard, CES or LES functions permit much more flexibility.

Compensating variation

A widely used measure of welfare change in CGE modelling. This measures the amount of income which would be required to compensate an individual, at the post-policy-change relative prices, to leave him or her at the initial level of welfare. (See also *equivalent variation*)

Counterfactual Equilibrium

An artificial equilibrium solution of the model, based on values of unknown parameters derived from calibration to the benchmark equilibrium data set, given specified changes in one or more policy regime.

Dynamic General Equilibrium Model

A model in which a sequence of static one-period equilibria are linked through time by assuming intertemporal optimisation on the part of agents. Base year changes in policy regime then lead to different sequences of counterfactual equilibria. For computational simplicity, expectations in dynamic models are frequently assumed to be myopic.

Extended Linear Expenditure System (ELES) Functions

The ELES utility function combines the instantaneous LES utility function (see later) with an additively separable intertemporal utility function which has a constant rate of time preference. Primarily it is used in dynamic general equilibrium structures to model the consumption-saving decision over time.

Equivalent variation

A widely used measure of welfare change in CGE modelling. It can be through of as the amount of income which would have to be taken from an individual, at the original (pre-policy-change) relative prices, to leave him or her at an equivalent level of welfare as in the pre-policy-change situation. (See also *compensating variation*)

Extraneous Elasticities

Elasticities (for CES functions etc.) used in the model calibration phase whose values have been determined exogenously. Typically, such values are obtained from 'central tendency' tables of elasticity estimates drawn from the appropriate literature.

Kakutani Fixed Point Theorem

A fixed point theorem concerned with point-to-set mappings of the unit simplex into itself. It is used to demonstrate the existence of a general equilibrium solution (fixed point) in models involving production activities, taxes, tariffs and trade restrictions.

Leontief Functions

Fixed-coefficient production functions implying zero elasticity of substitution between inputs. These are sometimes used to represent the intermediate stages of production in nested production activities.

Linear Expenditure System Functions (LES)

Demand (production) functions derived from LES utility functions do not enforce unitary own-price or income elasticity and permit non-zero cross-price elasticities. LES functions are the most flexible, but most heavily parameterised, of the functional forms in common use.

Merrill's Algorithm

A development of Scarf's algorithm allowing an arbitrary choice of starting point on the unit simplex (the initial equilibrium guess). The algorithm requires one more dimension than Scarf's algorithm, but can speed up computation time.

Nesting

A hierarchical system whereby utility (production) functions, such as CES, are embedded within other utility (production) functions up to a specified level. It is equivalent to assuming weak separability. In its simplest form, it permits (first level) substitution between a number of commodity groups, and then (second level) substitution within each individual group. Nesting can be used to expand the number of elasticity parameters available to calibrate to extraneous elasticity estimates.

Newton's Method

Often used as an alternative to Scarf-type algorithms to find fixed points (equilibrium solutions) in general equilibrium models. The method involves successive linear approximations to the underlying non-linear system and iterates towards equilibrium. Newton's method can be computationally efficient (it allows large initial adjustments from its starting point) however, unlike Scarf-type algorithms, convergence is not guaranteed.

Numéraire

For general equilibrium models in which only relative prices are important (when supply and demand functions are homogenous of degree zero), the price of any one factor or good in the model may be selected as a numéraire. All other prices are then deflated by the numéraire.

Parameterisation

In order that simulations can be run, all behavioural parameters in the model must have a numerical value. It is common for key parameters to be fixed using estimates from the econometric literature, or set by reference to the modeller's judgement. This process is referred to as parameterisation. (See also *calibration*).

Policy Appraisal

A pairwise comparison of benchmark and counterfactual equilibria used to analyse the impact of the specified policy changes. Normally, this involves constructing indices of changes in welfare levels (equivalent and compensating variations) or changes in the distribution of income (Gini coefficients).

Pre-selection

The process whereby a particular model structure is chosen. This builds upon the two factor framework common in public finance and international trade. This structure is attractive, partly for computational reasons, partly because it helps ensure consistency between the theoretical framework and numerical model. The absence of diagnostic tests in CGE modelling means that pre-selection is largely a matter of judgement.

R.A.S. Adjustment

A data adjustment technique used in the preparation of a benchmark data set to impose mutual consistency between inconsistent data (for instance, when observed household incomes do not equal total expenditures). Row-and-column sum constraints are imposed on a data matrix through a series of alternating operations on its rows and columns. Row constraints are first satisfied, then column constraints, and so on until a consistent matrix is produced. If the data matrix is dense, convergence is guaranteed.

Replication Check

Subsequent to model calibration, the replication check is used to establish that the derived model parameters are such that the benchmark equilibrium data set is still an equilibrium solution of the model. If the replication check fails then a programming error must exist.

Scarf's Algorithm

An early search algorithm used to find fixed points (equilibrium solutions) in general equilibrium models. Providing a fixed point exists, as can be established using the Brouwer / Kakutani theorem, the algorithm is non-cycling and guaranteed to converge to this point.

Sheppard's Lemma

An example of the envelope theorem. It states that the cost-minimising input vector is given by the vector of derivatives of the cost function with respect to the input prices.

Simplex

An n-dimensional geometrical figure in $n+1$ variables which consists of $n+1$ vertices and all the interconnecting line segments, polygonal faces etc. A unit simplex is such that at any point of the simplex, the sum of the values of all the variables is one. For $n = 2$, the simplex is represented by a triangular surface.

Social Accounting Matrix (SAM)

A square data matrix with identically labelled rows and columns. There is one row and column per agent (consumer, factor, producer) in the economy. A matrix element represents payments from the column agent to the row agent such that each row gives the agent's incomes and each column its expenditures. SAMs are constructed so as to satisfy the accounting identity that total income equals total expenditure for each agent (column and row sums are equal). A 'rest of the world' agent may be included so that this is satisfied. General equilibrium models can be formulated to exploit the SAM structure; such that there is a one-to-one relationship between the elements of the SAM and the behavioural equations in the model. By construction, the SAM then provides a consistent benchmark equilibrium data set for the model, from which calibration can proceed.

Two-Sector General Equilibrium Model

A simple form of general equilibrium model which assumes two commodities, two producers and two factors of production. Although a two sector model involves production, its unique structure allows Brouwer's theorem to be applied when proving the existence of an equilibrium solution (this is also very relevant to the computation of an equilibrium solution). Despite its simplicity, this model is widely used in the applied fields of taxation and trade. Also, much of the available data (such as national accounts data, input-output data) is in a form consistent with the two-sector modelling framework.

Van der Laan and Talman's Algorithm

A development of Scarf's algorithm allowing an arbitrary choice of starting point on the unit simplex (the initial equilibrium guess). Unlike Merrill's algorithm, the dimensionality required is the same as that of Scarf's algorithm, making it computationally faster.

Appendix B: Hardware and Software for CGE Modelling

Hardware

An important issue for the applied modeller is the amount of computing power required to solve a general equilibrium model. As a simple rule, as the dimension of the model increases, the more memory is required to hold the model, and the longer is the execution time (the slower is the convergence to an approximate equilibrium point). This is true irrespective of the choice of solution algorithm. Also, as the degree of model non-linearity increases, then other things being equal, execution times are lengthened. Thus, it is important that a computer with a large amount of RAM and fast CPU be available to the user. This is particularly the case if the model is going to be solved for a large number of counterfactual equilibria.

If attention is restricted to small scale models with simple structures, then these requirements can be of less concern. As an example, if the Shoven and Whalley (1984) two-good, two-factor, two-consumer model is calibrated and subsequently solved for one counterfactual equilibrium (involving a tax on one of the factors) using programs written in GAMS code on a 16Mhz CPU, 4Mb RAM PC-286, then the total compilation and execution time is approximately 29 seconds. In comparison, the same procedure takes around 5 seconds on a 50Mhz CPU, 4Mb RAM PC-486. Although the faster machine performs the task six times faster, the saving in computing time, in absolute terms, is very small. In a similar vein, for small scale problems the choice of solution algorithm is a much less critical issue. On the other hand, large scale models which involve many sectors and non-linearities can take hours, or perhaps days, of computing time to solve, even on very fast machines. On slow machines the amount of time required may then become infeasibly large.

Until the early 1980s, applied general equilibrium modelling was performed exclusively using mainframe computing facilities. Up to this time, microcomputers were insufficiently powerful or flexible enough to process even small scale models. However, the very rapid development in microchip technology over the last decade (in particular the developments in parallel processing and mathematical co-processing technology which have vastly increased the speed with which numerical operations can be performed) has led to the great majority of applied general equilibrium modelling now being undertaken on microcomputers. Only for exceedingly large models (those involving perhaps tens of thousands of variables) are mainframe facilities still necessary.

Software

As remarked above, early applied general equilibrium analysis was undertaken solely on mainframe installations. As such, the software available for programming the model structure was limited to that supported by the installation. Typically, this meant that the models had to be programmed in one of the high-level languages, the most widely used being FORTRAN. Solution algorithms were either also purpose written by the user, or taken from a sophisticated mathematical subroutine library, such as FORTRAN NAG (Numerical Algorithms Group) which includes a large variety of different numerical equation solving routines. Fairly obviously, this approach to modelling demanded that the modeller possess a significant level of programming expertise. Also, by its nature, such 'in-house' software tended to be very much problem-specific, making future model developments, in the form of generalisations or improvements, relatively difficult to incorporate (even supposing the appropriate solution software was widely available). In a similar fashion, such software was, to a large extent, also author-specific in that in that it was not generally written in such a manner that made it straightforward for users other than its author to apply without a good deal of prior familiarisation.

Today, some applied general equilibrium modellers still use 'in-house' software but there are an increasingly large number of proprietary mathematical software packages available for microcomputers which permit general equilibrium models to be programmed and solved in a much simpler fashion than was previously possible. Many of these packages are of a fairly flexible nature, allowing the analysis of a wide variety of statistical as well as mathematical problems, and have a variety of non-linear optimisation routines built into them. Others, however, are much more specifically tailored to the solution of non-linear mathematical programming problems and, within this, some are explicitly written for the solution of general equilibrium models. In fact, one of the current challenges in the field of applied general equilibrium modelling seems to be the creation of software that will make it simpler and faster to construct and solve these models, and several such packages are presently in development.

As a rule, the software packages which are purpose built for solving general equilibrium problems make model programming much easier than the less specific packages. However, they tend to be quite restrictive as regards the choice of functional forms which comprise the model. The less dedicated packages may require considerably more effort from the modeller in terms of programming, bench-testing, and error checking, but have the advantage that, in principle at least, they do not constrain the choice of functional forms.

General combined mathematical and statistical software packages can sometimes be inadequate for solving large scale general equilibrium systems due to the relative inefficiency of their inbuilt optimisation algorithms, although for problems with a small number of variables (say fifty or less) they can perform quite adequately. For the larger or more complex problems either mathematical programming packages or specific general equilibrium packages tend to be used.

The following sections list and discuss some of the properties of software currently being employed by applied general equilibrium modellers. Direct comparison between the various packages is made quite difficult by the substantial differences in the size and structure of the models they can accommodate, the way that data input is handled and the model solution procedures. Table 3.5 provides a summary of the available software for handling CGE modelling directly.

General Mathematical and Statistical Software

GAUSS

GAUSS is a self-contained mathematical and statistical programming language. Within the GAUSS syntax, the basic unit of analysis is a matrix, rather than a scalar as is the case with FORTRAN , PASCAL and C etc. This means that many mathematical operations that would involve complicated multiple loop coding in these other languages can be written in GAUSS as a single index-free statement which closely resembles its algebraic form. For instance, to multiply a matrix **X** by another matrix **Y**, irrespective of the matrix dimensions the GAUSS statement is simply **X*Y**; to invert **X** the statement is simply INV(**X**).

Because of the multivariate nature of general equilibrium models, involving simultaneous transformations on a number of variables, GAUSS is a highly appropriate language in which to code these models. Also, because GAUSS statements resemble their algebraic form, checking that functional forms etc. have been correctly specified is made fairly easy (this is most certainly not the case with languages like FORTRAN). Further, GAUSS allows sophisticated data manipulation and data can be read into GAUSS from a wide variety of different formats. The base GAUSS package contains no pre-written algorithms which can be used to solve general equilibrium models; however there are optional applications modules which contain algorithms for numerically solving simultaneous non-linear equations.

The current PC compatible (MS-DOS) release of GAUSS is version 3.0 GAUSS-386, which requires a 386 or 486 CPU with a 387 compatible maths co-processor and at least 4 Mb RAM. Matrix size (workspace) is limited only by the amount of available RAM and so manipulation of very large data sets is possible. Also available is GAUSS-386 VM which uses expanded memory allowing the workspace to expand up to the size of the hard disk. A UNIX version of GAUSS is in development.

MATHEMATICA

Mathematica is also a mathematical programming language and statistical data analysis system. It shares with GAUSS the ability to express matrix operations as single statements. However, as well as performing numerical computations, it also performs symbolic computation, allowing algebraic formulas to be manipulated. In particular, it can expand and factor rational expressions and find algebraic solutions to systems of equations. Although most general equilibrium models do not possess algebraic solutions, these symbolic capabilities may still be of considerable value when attempting to simplify a model prior to numerical solution. Mathematica also has inbuilt algorithms for the numerical solution of systems of algebraic equations and for finding (univariate) fixed points.

There are versions of Mathematica available for many different operating systems including Apple Macintosh, MS-DOS (386), VMS and UNIX. A minimum of 5 Mb of RAM is recommended to run Mathematica.

TABLE 3.5 SOFTWARE CURRENTLY AVAILABLE FOR CGE MODELLING

Name	Type	Sponsor	Supplier/contact
ASAP	SAM-based, non-linear equation solving	Overseas Development Administration, UK	ODA
GAMS	Non-linear programming	Commercial	GAMS Development Corp., 1217 Potomac St NW, Washington DC 20007, USA
GEMPACK	Solver for large linear models	Industries Commission, Canberra, Australia	IMPACT, Monash Univ., Clayton, Victoria, Australia
MAQM (Maquette)	SAM-based, flexible fixed point algorithm	OECD, World Bank	Prof. J. de Melo, The World Bank, 1818H St NW, Washington DC 20433, USA
MPS/GE	User-friendly; used with GAMS, handles CES, LES etc. directly	Commercial	GAMS Development Corp., 1217 Potomac St NW, Washington DC 20007, USA

GAMS

GAMS (General Algebraic Modelling System) is perhaps the most widely used of all the software packages for the computation of general equilibrium models, in spite of the fact that it is not specifically dedicated to this particular task. It is intended primarily for the construction and solution of linear and non-linear mathematical programming problems and, as such, possesses none of the statistical capabilities of the previous packages (these being redundant where applied general equilibrium analysis is concerned).

What makes GAMS useful to the applied general equilibrium modeller, however, is its ability to handle very large and complex problems and the fact that sets of simultaneous non-linear equations can be regarded as a special case of a non-linear mathematical programming problem and solved appropriately. Also, it is flexible enough to perform all the necessary data manipulations that are needed to calibrate parameters and initialise variables for the solution algorithm.

The syntax of GAMS allows a variety of data transformations and matrix operations to be written in a single algebraic statement but unlike, for instance the GAUSS syntax, element indexation cannot in general be avoided, although it is quite straightforward to perform. In fact, if different operations are to be carried out on different elements of vector or matrix, as is often the case, then ease of indexation becomes an important consideration. Also the number of inbuilt operators is much smaller (though many of GAUSS's inbuilt operators are in fact surplus to requirements for general equilibrium analysis). The reason for this is that GAMS is not really intended as a fully flexible programming language in itself, but rather as a means for representing a number of mathematical programming problems in a consistent and concise algebraic form. In addition, these problems are expressible independently of the solution algorithm, so that different solution algorithms can be employed without altering the algebraic representation of the problem in any way.

The basic structure of all GAMS models can be written in the following way:

1) Definition of sets of exogenous variables and assignment of members.
2) Assignment of parameter values to set members.
3) Definition of endogenous variables (solution variables).
4) Definition of model equations, constraints and objective function (as functions of the exogenous and endogenous variables).
5) Instruction to optimise the objective function in terms of the endogenous variables.

For general equilibrium models, there is no objective function to optimise because such models are defined entirely in terms of strict equalities (there are no inequality constraints). Since GAMS requires an objective function to be present, however, an arbitrary dummy objective function is defined in step (4). The purpose of this is to 'fool' GAMS into believing the dummy function is being optimised, whereas, in reality, the GAMS optimisation algorithm will simply solve the system of model equations in (4) for the endogenous variables.

Particular solution algorithms, or solvers, are supplied optionally with GAMS. It supports a large number of general-purpose licensed solvers for non-linear mathematical programming problems, including MINOS 5 (Murtagh and Saunders (1987)) and CONOPT (Drud (1985)), as well as some application-specific solvers. The basic GAMS package is supplied only with a linear program solver known as BDMLP; thus for applied general equilibrium modelling, separate solvers need to be purchased. An applications library is also available, which includes a number of examples of applied general equilibrium models.

The current release of GAMS is version 2.25. The MS-DOS PC version requires a 386 or 486 CPU with a 387 compatible mathematics co-processor, and a minimum of 4 Mb RAM is recommended (although 2 Mb may be sufficient to solve small models). This version also uses 32-bit addressing available with 386 and 486 CPUs. UNIX and (mainframe) CMS versions of GAMS are also available. There are some limits on the size of model GAMS can accommodate that depend, amongst many other factors, on the choice of solver. However, these should be not be so restrictive that any practically tractable general equilibrium model would run into workspace problems.

Applied General Equilibrium Software[1]

HERCULES

HERCULES (High level Economic Representation for Creation and Use of Large Economywide Systems) is a menu-driven software system for constructing and solving applied general equilibrium models that are based on a social accounting

---

1 A detailed appraisal of ASAP VI, MAQM, MPS/GE and GEMPACK V.4.2.02 is given in Harrigan (1993).

matrix (SAM). An introduction to the properties of SAMs is given in King (1981), and guidelines for the construction of SAMs are given in Keuning and Ruijter (1989). Basically, the variables and equations of a general equilibrium model can be structured in such a way so they fit very conveniently into the SAM framework and subsequently can use the SAM as a database This involves an alternative representation to the standard general equilibrium model, whereby the mathematical model is formulated in terms of behavioural equations and agents. Thorbecke (1985) gives an overview of the relationship between general equilibrium models and SAMs.

A feature of the HERCULES system is that it employs certain 'hard-wired' functional forms. These include Leontief, Cobb-Douglas, LES, CES and 2-level CES along with their associated first order optimality conditions. The reasoning behind this is that difficulties can be encountered when defining the model equations. This arises because the equations used in these models are often derived from quite complex underlying functional forms (such as CES functions) and the first order optimality conditions, and derivation (let alone programming) of these expressions is an error-prone activity, so that it is considerably more convenient for the modeller if this stage of modelling procedure is carried out automatically within the system. The MPS/GE and MAQM packages also share this feature.

Model parameters (such as share and scale parameters) for the hard wired utility and production functions are calibrated automatically within HERCULES, using the assumption that the SAM database represents a benchmark equilibrium data set. Exogenous parameters, such as elasticities and policy parameters need to be supplied by the user prior to calibration, however. Unlike MPS/GE, HERCULES does not handle complementarity problems associated with activity analysis since this is fairly difficult to combine with the SAM-based modelling structure.

The modelling infrastructure and solution algorithms for HERCULES are provided by GAMS. However, it is incompatible with the more recent versions of GAMS. Further information on HERCULES and GAMS can be found in Drud and Kendrick (1986).

MPS/GE

MPS/GE (Mathematical Programming Software / General Equilibrium) is a sequential complementarity algorithm used to solve general equilibrium models. It is based around the mathematical programming approach to general equilibrium modelling developed by Scarf and Hansen (1973). The models may be expressed in activity analysis form as well as the conventional Walrasian format.

MPS/GE has its own programming language which allows an economical representation of even quite complex models. The models and data are input using batch command files. Unlike ASAP, however, MPS/GE has no interactive mode.

Production and demand structures can be written in a shorthand notation since functional forms such as CES, CET, Cobb-Douglas and Leontief are 'hard wired' into the system (taxes on inputs and subsidies can be similarly treated). The family of inbuilt functions is sufficiently flexible to allow the possibility of joint production and an activity analysis representation of technologies. Substitution possibilities can be further expanded through, for example, nesting CES functions. Model calibration is carried out automatically although, unlike the SAM-based systems, there is no inbuilt requirement that the model data set represents a benchmark equilibrium before this can proceed. Replication checks can also be carried out automatically. Dynamic models can also be solved within MPS/GE.

MPS/GE runs under MS-DOS, VMS and interfaces with GAMS (it is available as a separately purchased solver). It is supplied with an applications library which includes the Cameroon model. The PC version requires a mathematics co-processor but the current release does not make use of the extended memory facilities available on most modern PCs. MPS/GE can accommodate problems with up to 300 variables, which means that it is not really suited to solving large dynamic GE models.

ASAP

ASAP (A Social Accounting Package), in common with HERCULES and MAQM, is based on the SAM approach to general equilibrium modelling. It is basically a high level programming environment for model specification, which uses a SAM as a database, and incorporates a non linear equation solving algorithm. The command syntax is matrix based, and has similar features to that of GAUSS and SAS/IML in terms of the way matrix operations are performed and submatrices are defined.

ASAP handles linear models (such as social accounting and/or input-output models) very well. It is easy to structure such models within ASAP, it can accommodate large models, and it solves them relatively quickly. However, it is much less suited to the solution of large or highly non-linear general equilibrium models. There are no 'hard wired' production or utility functions and the ASAP syntax is not ideal for performing the necessary non-linear transformations. Models are not calibrated automatically and there is no built in replication check. Further, its non-linear equation solving algorithm is comparatively simplistic. This, however, only reflects the fact that ASAP was not explicitly developed with such complex models in mind.

ASAP runs under MS-DOS, requires a minimum of 640Kb RAM, but does not require a mathematics co-processor (although one is recommended). It can accommodate models of up to 1500 variables with 300 SAM accounts and is capable of both interactive and batch mode operation. Also, ASAP allows data to be input from a wide variety of spreadsheet programs.

MAQM

MAQM (Maquette) is an environment for constructing and solving models belonging to the Maquette class (Bourguignon, Branson and de Melo (1991)). Model specification, data entry (which includes SAM format data) and model solution are all menu controlled so that no equations need to be user supplied. MAQM prompts the user for model dimensions (number of products, consumers etc.), and allows the user to select from a number of hard wired functional forms (such as Leontief and CES) and model closure options using multi-level menus. With the model specified in this way, automatic checks are made to test whether the data satisfies the benchmark equilibria. If necessary, MAQM can perform RAS adjustment. Calibration and replication checking are also carried out within MAQM. Counterfactual analysis is then performed simply by imposing new values on certain parameters, and dynamic simulation can also be undertaken. MAQM uses a very flexible fixed point algorithm to compute the model equilibrium. This allows starting values to be set and solution tolerances to be defined.

MAQM runs under MS-DOS, requiring a 386 or 486 CPU with a 387 compatible mathematics co-processor. At least 1 Mb RAM is needed. It can handle models with up to 18 commodities (activities), 6 transactor types, 1 capital asset and 6 types of labour. Dynamic simulation can be performed up to 12 periods ahead. An example general equilibrium model is provided with the MAQM documentation.

GEMPACK

GEMPACK (General Equilibrium Modelling PACKage) is a general-purpose software package for building and simulating general equilibrium models. It is particularly suited to handling very large models and includes features which allow such models to be condensed to manageable dimensions. GEMPACK is the package used in the Australian ORANI model of Dixon *et al.* (1982) (a model which itself contained several million equations and variables). A large variety of different closure rules may be specified. Counterfactual analysis is carried out by replacing the non-linear equation system with the linearised approximation due to Johansen (1960) and implemented via the solution algorithm SAGEM, which calls Harwell Laboratories (AEA Technologies) sparse matrix routines. Model specification and interface with SAGEM is made through TABLO, a high level algebraic modelling language which requires that the user supply analytical expressions for the linearised model.

Although GEMPACK is very flexible, the way the model must be specified is relatively involved, which could make it unsuitable for users without some experience of programming. The current release of GEMPACK is version 4.2.02 (April 1991) and is available for MS-DOS, Apple, UNIX and VMS operating systems. A demonstration version and further information is supplied with Dixon *et al.* (1992).

Appendix C: GAMS Code for the Shoven and Whalley Model[1]

This appendix lists the GAMS® code to accompany the example of a simple general equilibrium analysis laid out in Chapter 2. The code itself is given in the boxes; all the remaining text is explanatory. GAMS permits lengthy comment statements to be made within the program, but these have not been included here.

The Benchmark Data Set

The basic model is constructed assuming two factors of production, labour and capital; two production sectors, manufactured and non-manufactured; and two types of consumer group, a rich group and a poor group. The GAMS code used to specify this structuring of the economy is as follows:

```
SETS
   F              factors              /LABOUR, CAPITAL/,
   S              sectors              /MAN, NONMAN/,
   C              consumer group       /RICH, POOR/ ;
ALIAS (F, FF), (S, SS), (C, CC);
```

The SET(S) command defines the dimensions of the model in terms of named sets (matrices), and specifies the names given to the elements within each set. In the example above the sets are defined as F, S, and C. GAMS recognises that the set F, for example, has two elements, LABOUR and CAPITAL (so that there is no need to declare the dimensions of a set). Note that GAMS does not allow variable names to contain spaces, so that 'NON MAN' would be inadmissible ('MAN' would be treated as a text comment); 'NONMAN' or 'NON-MAN' are acceptable. The set is delineated by the '/' characters. The entries 'factors' etc. are *text*, used for internal documentation (and are not essential). The ALIAS command allows us to use multiple names for the same set; that is, set FF has been defined to be the same as set F. This is useful when it is necessary to access a set which is under the control of a function.

1 The GAMS code in Appendix C was written by Eric Hutton, CSIER, Department of Economics, University of Western Ontario.

The benchmark data set can be read into GAMS in a number of ways. The PARAMETER assignment is illustrated here. The parameters are again defined as sets, the index (or indices) of the sets being specified in parentheses, and the elements of the set delineated by '/'. Thus the set BENPRDN is a vector indexed on S, and BENPRDN(MAN) has been set equal to 34.898. BENFACDEM is a matrix indexed on S and F, and BENFACDEM(MAN, LABOUR) has been set to 26.366. The entries 'production by sector' etc. are again comments for internal documentation. Note that factor taxes are all assumed to be zero in the base situation.

```
PARAMETERS
     BENPRDN(S)                    production by sector
          /MAN                           34.898
           NONMAN                        59.439/,
     BENFACDEM(S, F)               factors used by sector
        /MAN.LABOUR                      26.366
         NONMAN.LABOUR                   33.634
         MAN.CAPITAL                      8.532
         NONMAN.CAPITAL                  25.805/,
     ELASP(S)                 elasticity of substitution in production
        /MAN                              2.000
         NONMAN                           0.500/
     ELASC(C)                 elasticity of substitution in consumption
        /RICH                             1.500
         POOR                             0.750/,
     ENDOW(C, F)                  consumer factor endowment
        /RICH.CAPITAL                    34.337
         RICH.LABOUR                      0.000
         POOR.CAPITAL                     0.000
         POOR.LABOUR                     60.000/,
```

BENDEMAND(C, S)	consumer commodity demand
/RICH.MAN	16.110
RICH.NONMAN	18.277
POOR.MAN	18.782
POOR.NONMAN	41.212/,
TAXSHR(C)	proportion of tax revenues to consumer group
/RICH	0.400
POOR	0.600/,
FACTAX(S, F)	factor tax by sector (in base case)
/MAN.CAPITAL	0.000
MAN.LABOUR	0.000
NONMAN.CAPITAL	0.000
NONMAN.LABOUR	0.000/;

Calibration to the Benchmark Data Set

With the equilibrium data set entered as above, the remaining unknown parameter values can be determined through calibration. The first order conditions for cost-minimisation yield values of the distribution parameters in production and the demand share parameters are similarly obtained. The production scale parameter is determined from the zero profit equilibrium condition. We declare the unknown parameter, then assign it a value according to the appropriate formula.

The initial statements in the following box identify the three sets of parameters which are to be specified. Each element of each set is then specified in turn. Note that the '/' term in this context indicates division and that 'x**y' indicates x^y. Finally, the ';' indicates the completion of an assignment.

```
PARAMETERS
  DISTN(S, F)                     production distribution parameter
  SHARE(C, S)                     demand share parameter
  SCALE(S)                        production scale parameter ;
  DISTN(S, "CAPITAL") = (((BENFACDEM(S, "CAPITAL"))**(1 / ELASP(S)) *
                  (1 + FACTAX(S, "CAPITAL"))) /
                  ((BENFACDEM(S, "LABOUR"))**(1 / ELASP(S)) *
                  (1 + FACTAX(S, "LABOUR")))) /
                  (1+(((BENFACDEM(S, "CAPITAL"))**(1 / ELASP(S)) *
                  (1 + FACTAX(S, "CAPITAL"))) /
                  ((BENFACDEM(S, "LABOUR"))**(1 / ELASP(S)) *
                  (1 + FACTAX(S,"LABOUR"))))) ;
   DISTN(S, "LABOUR") = 1 - DISTN(S, "CAPITAL") ;
   SCALE(S) = BENPRDN(S) / ((SUM(F,DISTN(S, F)*BENFACDEM(S, F) **
                  ((ELASP(S)-1) / ELASP(S) ** (ELASP(S) / (ELASP(S)-1))) ;
   SHARE(C, "MAN") = (BENDEMAND(C, "MAN") /
           BENDEMAND(C, "NONMAN")) / (1 + (BENDEMAND(C, "MAN") /
           BENDEMAND(C, "NONMAN"))) ;
   SHARE(C, "NONMAN") = 1 - SHARE(C, "MAN") ;
```

Model Declaration

Given our fully specified model (including all parameter values obtained through calibration), we verify the results obtained prior to examining a counterfactual equilibria. The replication check verifies whether, given the derived parameter values, the benchmark data set does indeed represent an equilibrium solution. To perform the replication check, we first specify the model within GAMS. This involves declaring the solution variables and the equations to be used in solving for these variables.

```
POSITIVE VARIABLES
        P(S)                    commodity price by sector
        W(F)                    factor prices
        TAXREV                  tax revenue
        PRDN(S)                 production by sector
        DEMAND(C, S)            consumer demand for commodity
        FACDEM(S, F)            factor demanded by sector
        M(C)                    income by household ;
VARIABLE
        DUMMY                   dummy objective value ;
```

The POSITIVE VARIABLES statements restricts the solution algorithm, or solver, to solutions which yield positive values for these variables. We use the VARIABLE statement to define a false objective variable. This fools the solver into believing it is performing an non-linear programming task with some particular objective function.

To solve for each of these variables, we need to specify the conditions underlying equilibrium in the model. To create an equation containing variables we use the EQUATIONS statement, which gives a name to each equation.

```
EQUATIONS
    PRDFUN(S)               production function
    FDEMFN(S, F)            factor demand function
    NCOME(C)                consumer income
    CDEMFN(C, S)            commodity demand function
    FACMKT(F)               factor demands equals supply
    CMDMKT(S)               commodity demand equals supply
    ZERPRO(S)               zero profit condition
    GVTBGT                  government budget equation
    DUMOBJ                  dummy objective function ;
```

Once declared in this way, explicit functional forms for each equation must be given. Note that when defining a functional form (as opposed to assigning a value to a variable), the notation '=E=' is required.

```
PRDFUN(S)                 production function
  PRDN(S) =E= SCALE(S) * SUM(F, DISTN(S, F) * (FACDEM(S, F) **
    ((ELASP(S) - 1) / ELASP(S)))) ** (ELASP(S) / (ELASP(S) - 1)) ;

FDEMFN(S,F)               factor demand function
  FACDEM(S,F) =E= (1 / SCALE(S)) * PRDN(S) * (DISTN(S, F) +
    ((SUM(FF, DISTN(S,FF)) - DISTN(S,F)) * ((DISTN(S,F) *
    (SUM(FF, W(FF) * (1 + FACTAX(S, FF))) - W(F) * (1 + FACTAX(S, F)))) /
    ((SUM(FF, DISTN(S, FF)) - DISTN(S, F)) * W(F) *
    (1 + FACTAX(S, F)))) ** (1 - ELASP(S)))) ** (ELASP(S) / (1 - ELASP(S))) ;

INCOME(C)                 consumer income
  M(C) =E= SUM(F, W(F)*ENDOW(C, F)) + TAXSHR(C)*TAXREV ;

CDEMFN(C, S)              commodity demand function
  DEMAND(C, S) =E= (SHARE(C, S) * M(C)) / ((P(S) ** ELASC(C)) *
    (SUM(SS, (SHARE(C, SS)*(P(SS)**(1 - ELASC(C))))))) ;

FACMKT(F)                 factor demands equals supply
  SUM(S, FACDEM(S, F)) =E= SUM(C, ENDOW(C, F)) ;

CMDMKT(S)                 commodity demand equals supply
  SUM(C, DEMAND(C, S)) =E= PRDN(S) ;

ZERPRO(S)                 zero profit condition
  P(S)*PRDN(S) =E= SUM(F, W(F)*(1+FACTAX(S, F))*FACDEM(S, F)) ;

GVTBGT                    government budget equation
  SUM(C, TAXSHR(C)*TAXREV)=E=SUM((S, F),FACTAX(S, F)
    *W(F)*FACDEM(S, F)) ;

DUMOBJ                    dummy objective function
  DUMMY =E= SUM(S, PRDN(S)) ;
```

Having stated all the model equations in this way, we group them using the MODEL statement. This statement indicates to the solver which equations are to be used to solve a particular problem.

```
MODEL
        CGE /ALL/ ;
```

CGE is simply a name attached to the model. The ALL statement tells the solver to take into account all the equations which have been declared to date (if required, subsets of equations can be individually specified).

To avoid division by zero problems, lower bounds on variables can be specified.

```
PRDN.LO(S) = 0.1 ;
DEMAND.LO(C, S) = 0.1 ;
FACDEM.LO(S, F) = 0.1 ;
P.LO(S) = 0.1 ;
W.LO(F) = 0.1 ;
```

Replication Check

The next step solves the model. To help the solver find an equilibrium the starting values for the algorithm are the original values from the benchmark equilibrium; all prices have been assigned a value of unity in the benchmark. The suffix L on the solution variables is required if its value is to be displayed (this is not required for displaying the values of parameters).

```
PRDN.L(S) = BENPRDN(S) ;
DEMAND.L(C, S) = BENDEMAND(C, S) ;
FACDEM.L(S, F) = BENFACDEM(S,F) ;
P.L(S) = 1.000 ;
W.L(F) = 1.000 ;
SOLVE CGE USING NLP MAXIMIZING DUMMY ;
DISPLAY W.L, P.L, PRDN.L, M.L, DEMAND.L, FACDEM.L ;
DISPLAY DISTN, SCALE, SHARE ;
```

The SOLVE command informs the solver to find the solution to the model CGE using the NLP (Non-linear Programming) routine. The solver then attempts to maximise DUMMY subject to a number of constraints which are actually strict equalities. In doing so, it simply solves the system of equations we are interested in.

To confirm that the solution replicates the benchmark equilibrium, we check that the values of the variables displayed after the SOLVE command match their benchmark counterparts. As this is the case, we may accept the calibrated values of the unknown parameters (shown in the second DISPLAY command) as being correct.

Counterfactual Analysis

As the benchmark equilibrium is confirmed, we can proceed to simulate a counterfactual equilibrium. In keeping with Shoven and Whalley, we assume a 50% tax on capital use in the manufacturing sector and set:

```
FACTAX("MAN", "CAPITAL") = 0.500 ;
```

In the role of numéraire, we include the constraint that the wage rate of labour equals unity. This does not affect equilibrium values, but simply prices all goods and factors relative to labour. To impose this additional constraint, we use the suffix FX, which fixes the value of the variable concerned.

```
W.FX("LABOUR") = 1.000 ;
```

Having set up the counterfactual case in this way, we solve for the equilibrium values using exactly the same procedure as for the replication of the benchmark equilibrium, and display the values of the relevant variables (including tax revenue).

```
SOLVE CGE USING NLP MAXIMIZING DUMMY ;
DISPLAY W.L, P.L, PRDN.L, M.L, DEMAND.L, FACDEM.L, TAXREV.L ;
```

A comparison of the benchmark and counterfactual equilibria, measured in terms of welfare gains and losses, can be made using a Hicksian equivalent variation. It should be noted that the formula for the equivalent variation given in the following box is appropriate if, and only if, utility is of a linear homogenous form.

```
PARAMETER
HEV(C)                          Hicksian equivalent variation ;
   HEV(C) = ((((SUM(S, (SHARE(C, S) ** (1 / ELASC(C))) *
          DEMAND.L(C, S) ** ((ELASC(C)-1)/ELASC(C))))) ** (ELASC(C) /
          (ELASC(C)-1))) - ((SUM(S, (SHARE(C, S)**(1 / ELASC(C))) *
          (BENDEMAND(C, S) ** ((ELASC(C)-1) / ELASC(C)))))
          ** (ELASC(C) / (ELASC(C)-1)))) / ((SUM(S, (SHARE(C, S)
          ** (1/ELASC(C))) * (BENDEMAND(C, S) ** ((ELASC(C)-1) /
          ELASC(C))))) ** (ELASC(C) / (ELASC(C)-1)))) *
          SUM(F, ENDOW(C, F)) ;
DISPLAY HEV ;
```

Appendix D: Bibliography of the CGE Literature

There is a vast, and growing, literature on CGE modelling. Our report has only referred in any detail to a fraction of the literature. In this appendix we provide a more comprehensive bibliography.

Armington, P. (1969), 'A theory of demand for products distinguished by place of production', *IMF Staff Papers*, **16**, 159-78.

Arnott, R.J. and MacKinnon, J.G. (1977), 'The effects of the property tax: a general equilibrium simulation', *Journal of Urban Economics* , **4**, 389-407.

Arrow, K.J., and Debreu, G. (1954), 'Existence of an equilibrium for a competitive economy', *Econometrica*, **22**, 265-90.

Arrow, K.J., and Hahn, F. (1971), *General Competitive Analysis,* San Francisco, Holden-Day.

Auerbach, A.J. and Kotlikoff, L.J. (1983), 'National savings, economic welfare, and the structure of taxation', in *Behavioural Simulation Methods in Tax Policy Analysis* (M. Feldstein, ed.), Chicago, University of Chicago Press.

Auerbach, A.J., Kotlikoff, L.J. and Skinner, J. (1983), 'The efficiency gain from dynamic tax reform', *International Economic Review*, **24**, 81-100.

Baldwin, R. (1992), 'Measurable dynamic gains from trade', *Journal of Political Economy*, **100**, 162-174.

Ballard, C.L. (1983), 'Evaluation of the consumption tax with dynamic general equilibrium models', unpublished Ph.D. dissertation, Stanford University.

Ballard, C.L. and Goulder, L.H (1982), 'Expectations in numerical general equilibrium models', *Research paper no. 31,* Stanford Workshop in the Microeconomics of Factor Markers, Stanford. CA, Department of Economics, Stanford University.

Ballard, C.L. and Goulder, L.H. (1982), 'Tax policy and consumer foresight: general equilibrium simulation study', Harvard Institute of Economic Research Discussion Paper No 940, Harvard University, December.

Ballard, C.L. and Goulder, L.H. (1985). 'Consumption taxes, consumer foresight. and welfare', in *New Developments in Applied General Equilibrium Analysis,* (J. Piggot and J. Whalley, eds), New York, Cambridge University Press.

Ballard, C.L., Fullerton, D., Shoven, J.B. and Whalley, J. (1985), *A General Equilibrium Model for Tax Policy Evaluation*, Chicago, University of Chicago Press.

Ballard, C.L., Shoven, J.B. and Whalley, J. (1982), 'The welfare costs of distortions in the U.S. tax system: a general equilibrium approach', *Working Paper No. 1043,* Cambridge, Mass., National Bureau of Economic Research

Ballard, C.L., Shoven, J.B. and Whalley, J. (1985), 'General equilibrium computations of the marginal welfare costs of taxes in the United States', *American Economic Review*, **75**, 128-137.

Ban, K. (1991), 'Energy conservation and economic performance in Japan: an econometric approach to CO2 emissions', Osaka University Economics Department Discussion Paper no. 112.

Barns, D.W., Edmonds, J.A. and Reilly, J.M. (1992), 'Use of the Edmonds-Reilly model to model energy related greenhouse gas emissions for inclusion in an OECD survey volume', *OECD Economics Department Working Papers*, **13**.

Becker, C.M., Mills, E.S. and Williamson, J.G. (1983), 'Public policy, urbanization and development: a computable general equilibrium model of the Indian economy', *Working Paper No. 83-W14,* Department of Economics, Vanderbilt University.

Bergman, L. (1989), *Tillväxt och miljö en Studie av Malkonflikter,* Bilaga 9 till Langtidsutredningen 1990, Finansdepartementet, Stockholm.

Bergman, L. (1990), 'Energy and environmental constraints on growth: a CGE modelling approach', *Journal of Policy Modelling*, **12**, 671-691.

Blitzer, C., Clark, P., and Taylor, L. (1975), *Economy-Wide Models and Development Planning,* London, Oxford University Press.

Blitzer, C., Eckaus, R.S., Lahiri, S. and Meeraus, A. (1990), 'A general equilibrium analysis of the effects of carbon emission restrictions on economic growth in a developing country', *Procedings of the Workshop on Economic/ Energy/Environmental Modelling for Climate Policy Analysis*, Washington DC.

Boadway, R, and Treddenick, J.M (1978), 'A general equilibrium computation of the effects of the Canadian tariff structure', *Canadian Journal of Economics* **11**, 424-46.

Boero, G., Clarke, R. and Winters, L.A. (1991), *The Macroeconomic Consequences of Controlling Greenhouse Gases: A Survey,* UK Department of the Environment, London.

Borges, A, and Goulder, L.H. (1984), 'Decomposing the impact of higher energy prices on long-term growth', in *Applied General Equilibrium Analysis,* (H.E. Scarf and J.B. Shoven, eds), New York, Cambridge University Press.

Borges, A. (1984), 'Tax reform in Portugal: a general equilibrium analysis of the introduction of a value added tax', *Working Paper 84-12,* INSEAD.

Bourguignon, F., Branson , W.H. and de Melo, J. (1991), 'Adjustment and income distribution: a micro-macro model for counterfactual analysis', *Journal of Development Economics*, **31**.

Bovenberg, A. L. (1983), 'Capital immobility, capital accumulation, and financial assets: theory in an applied general equilibrium framework', Berkeley, CA, University of California, Department of Economics.

Bovenberg, A.L. and Keller, W.J. (1981), 'Dynamics and nonlinearities in applied general equilibrium models', Central Bureau of Statistics, the Netherlands.

Brouwer, L.E.J. (1910), 'Uber eine eindeutige, stetige Transformationen von Flachen in sich', *Mathematische Annalen* , **67**, 176-80.

Brown, D.K. (1988), 'A computational analysis of the effects of the Tokyo Round negotiations on preferential trading arrangements', *Journal of International Economic Integration.*

Brown, D.K. (1989), 'Market structure, the exchange rate, and pricing behavior by firms: some evidence from computable general equilibrium trade models', *Weltwirtschaftliches Archiv.*

Brown, D.K. and Stern, R.M. (1989), 'Computable general equilibrium estimates of the gains from U.S.-Canada trade liberalization', in *Economic Aspects of Regional Trading Arrangements* (D. Greenaway, T. Hyclak and R.J. Thornton, eds), Harvester Wheatsheaf.

Brown, D.K., Deardorff, A.V. and Stern, R.M. (1992), 'A North American Free Trade Agreement: Analytical issues and Computational Assessment', *The World Economy,* **15**, 11-30.

Brown, F. and Whalley, J. (1980), 'General equilibrium evaluations of tariff-cutting proposals in the Tokyo Round and comparisons with more extensive liberalization of world trade', *Economic Journal*, **90**, 838-66.

Browning (1978), 'The burden of taxation', *Journal of Political Economy*, **86**, 649-71.

Burniaux, J-M., Martin, J.P., Nicoletti, G. and Oliveira Martins, J. (1991), 'The cost of policies to reduce global emissions of CO2: initial simulation results with GREEN', OECD Economics Department Working Paper no. 103.

Burniaux, J-M., Martin, J.P., Nicoletti, G. and Oliveira Martins, J. (1992a), 'The costs of international agreements to reduce CO_2 emissions', *European Economy,* (forthcoming).

Burniaux, J-M., Martin, J.P., Nicoletti, G. and Oliveira Martins, J. (1992b), 'Green - A multi-sector, multi-region dynamic general equilibrium model for quantifying the costs of curbing CO2 emissions: A technical manual', OECD Economics Department Working Paper no. 116.

Bye, T., Bye, B. and Lorentsen, L. (1989), 'Studies of industry, environment and energy towards 2000', Discussion Paper, Central Bureau of Statistics, Oslo.

Carrin, G.. Gunning, J.W. and Waelbroeck, J. (1983), 'A general equilibrium model for the world economy: some preliminary results', in *Global International Economic Models* (B. G. Hickman, ed.), Amsterdam, North-Holland.

CBO (Congressional Budget Office) (1990), *Carbon Charges*, Washington DC, US Government Printing Office.

Cecchini, P. *et al.* (1988), *The European Challenge: The Benefits of a Single Market*, Aldershot, Wildwood House.

Chichilnisky, G. Heal, G.M. and McLeod, D. (1983), 'Resources, trade and debt', mimeo, Columbia University.

Christensen, A. (1991), 'Stabilisation of CO_2 emissions: economic effects for Finland', Ministry of Finance Discussion Paper no. 29, Helsinki.

Clarete, R. and Whalley, J. (1986), 'Equilibrium in the Presence of Foreign Exchange Premia', University of Western Ontario.

Clements, K.W. (1980), 'A general equilibrium econometric model of an open economy', *International Economic Review*, **27**, 469-88.

Cline, W.R. (1989), 'Political Economy of the Greenhouse Effect', mimeo, IIE, Washington DC.

Cline, W.R. (1992), *The Economics of Global Warming,* Institute for International Economics, Washington.

Condon, T., Corbo, V. and Melo, J. de (1986), 'Industrial Organisation Implications of QR Trade Regimes: Evidence and Welfare Costs', Washington, D.C., World Bank.

Cox, D. and Harris, R. (1985), 'Trade liberalization and industrial organisation: some estimates for Canada', *Journal of Political Economy*, **93**, 115-45.

Cox, D. and Harris, R.G. (1992), 'North American Free Trade and its Implications for Canada', *The World Economy,* **15**, 31-44.

Dahl, J. Devarajan, S. and van Wijnbergen, S. (1986), 'Revenue Neutral Tariff Reform: Theory and an Application to Cameroon', Washington D.C.: World Bank.

de Melo, J. and Robinson, S (1985), 'Product Differentiation and Trade Dependence of the Domestic Price System in Computable General Equilibrium Trade Models', in *International Trade and Exchange Rates in the Late Eighties* (T. Peeters *et al* ., eds), Amsterdam, North Holland.

de Melo, J. and Robinson, S. (1989), 'Product Differentiation and the Treatment of Foreign Trade in Computable General Equilibrium models of Small Economies', *Journal of International Economics*.

de Melo, J. and Tarr, D.G. (1988), 'Welfare costs of U.S. quotas in textiles, steel and autos', mimeo, World Bank.

de Melo, J. and Urata S. (1986), 'The Influence of Increased Foreign Competition on Industrial Concentration and Profitability', *International Journal of Industrial Organisation,* **4**, 287-304.

de Melo, J.(1978), 'Estimating the costs of protection: a general equilibrium approach', *Quarterly Journal of Economics,* **42**, 209-26.

Dean, A. and Hoeller, P. (1992), 'Costs of reducing CO_2 emissions: evidence from six global models', OECD Economics Department Working Paper no. 122.

Deardorff, A.V. and Stern, R.M. (1981), 'A disaggregated model of world production and trade: an estimate of the impact of the Tokyo round', *Journal of Policy Modelling*, **3**, 127-52.

Deardorff, A.V. and Stern, R.M. (1985), *The Michigan model of world production and trade: theory and applications,*Cambridge, Ma., MIT Press.

Deardorff, A.V. and Stern, R.M. (1986), *The Michigan Model of World Trade and Production*, Cambridge, Ma., MIT Press.

Debreu, G. (1959), *Theory of Value,* New York, John Wiley.

Decaluwe, B. and Martens, A. (1986), 'CGE Modelling andDeveloping Economies: A Concise Empirical Survey of 56 Applications to 24 Countries', CRDE Study No. 1686, Montreal University.

Dervis, J. and Robinson, S. (1982), 'A General Equilibrium Analysis of the Causes of a Foreign Exchange Crisis: The Case of Turkey', *Weltwirtschaftliches Archiv,* **118**, 259-279.

Dervis, K., de Melo, J. and Robinson, S. (1981), 'General equilibrium analysis of foreign exchange shortages in a developing economy', *Economic Journal*, **91**, 891-906.

Dervis, K., de Melo, J. and Robinson, S. (1982), *General Equilibrium Models for Development Policy,* New York, Cambridge University Press.

Devarajan, S. (1988), 'Natural Resources and Taxation in Computable General Equilibrium Models of Developing Countries', *Journal of Policy Modelling,* **10**, 505-528.

Devarajan, S. and Robinson, S. (1983), 'Selected bibliography on computable general equilibrium models of developing countries', mimeo, Harvard and UC Berkeley.

Devarajan, S. Lewis, J. and Robinson, S. (1986), 'A Bibliography of Computable General Equilibrium (CGE) Models for Developing Countries', HHD Discussion Paper, No. 224, Cambridge, Massachusetts: Harvard University.

Dewatripont, M. and Michel, G. (1987), 'On Closure Rules, Homogeneity and Dynamics in Applied General Equilibrium Models', *Journal of Development Economics,* **26**, 65-76.

Dick, H., Gerker, E., Mayer, T. and Vincent, D. (1983), 'Stabilisation strategies in primary commodity exporting countries: a case study of Chile', *Journal of Development Economics.*, **15**, 47-75

Dinwiddy, C.L. and Teal, F.J. (1988), *The Two-Sector General Equilibrium Model: A New Approach*, Oxford, Philip Allan.

Dixon, P.B, Parmenter, B.R., Sutton, J. and Vincent, D. (1981), *ORANI: a MultiSectoral Model of the Australian Economy,* Amsterdam, North-Holland.

Dixon, P.B. (1992), *Notes and problems in applied general equilibrium economics*, Amsterdam North-Holland, forthcoming.

Dixon, P.B., Johnson, D.T., Marks, R.E., McLennan, P, Schodde, R. and Swan, P.L. (1989), 'The feasibility and implication for Australia of the adoption of the Toronto proposal for carbon dioxide emissions', Report to CRA Sydney.

Dixon, P.B., Parmenter, B.R. and Rimmer, R.J. (1984), 'Extending the ORANI model of the Australian economy: adding foreign investment to a miniature version', in *Applied General Equilibrium Analysis,* (H.E. Scarf and J.B. Shoven, eds), New York, Cambridge University Press.

Dixon, P.B., Parmenter, B.R., Sutton, J. and Vincent, D.P. (1982), *ORANI: A Multisectoral Model of the Australian Economy*, Amsterdam, North-Holland.

Drud, A. (1985), *HERCULES: a SAM-based system for general equilibrium modeling,* ARKI Consulting and Development, Bagsvaerd, Denmark.

Drud, A., Grais, W. and Pyatt, G. (1986), 'Macroeconomic modelling based on social accounting principles', *Journal of Policy Modeling*, **8**, 25-36.

Drud, A. and Kendrick, D. (1986), 'HERCULES - a system for large economy-wide models', Development Research Department, World Bank.

Dungan, D.P. (1980), 'An empirical multi-sectoral Walrasian-Keynesian model of the Canadian Economy', unpublished Ph.D. dissertation, Princeton University.

Eastman, H. and Stykolt, S. (1960), 'A model for the study of protected oligopolies', *Economic Journal*, **70**, 336-47.

Eastman, H. and Stykolt, S. (1967), *The Tariff and Competition in Canada*, Toronto, Macmillan.

Eaves, B.C. (1972), 'Homotopies for the computation of fixed points', *Mathematical Programming*, **3**, 1-22.

Eaves, B.C. (1974), 'Properly labelled simplexes', in *Studies in Optimisation,* MAA Studies in Mathematics 10, (G.B. Dantzig and B.C. Eaves, eds)

Edmonds, J.A. and Barns, D.W. (1990), 'Estimating the marginal cost of reducing global fossil fuel CO_2 emissions', mimeo, Pacific Northwest Laboratory, Washington D.C..

Edmonds, J.A. and Reilly, J.M (1983), 'Global energy and CO2 to the year 2000', *The Energy Journal,* **4**, 21-47.

Feenberg, D.R. and Rosen, H.S. (1983), 'Alternative tax treatment of the family: simulation methodology and results', in *Behavioral Simulation Methods in Tax Policy Analysis* (M. Feldstein, ed.), Chicago, University of Chicago Press.

Feldstein, M. and Feenberg, D.R. (1983). 'Alternative tax rules and personal saving incentives: microeconomic data and behavioral simulations', in *Behavioral Simulation Methods in Tax Policy Analysis* (M. Feldstein, ed.), Chicago, University of Chicago Press.

Feltenstein, A. (1980), 'A general equilibrium approach to the analysis of trade restrictions, with an application to Argentina', *International Monetary Fund Staff Papers,* **27**, 749-84.

Feltenstein, A. (1984), 'Money and bonds in a disaggregated open economy', in Applied *General Equilibrium Analysis* (H.E. Scarf and J.B. Shoven, eds), New York, Cambridge University Press.

Fisher, F. (1976), 'The stability of general equilibrium: results and problems', in *Essays in Economic Analysis* (M. Artis and E. Nobay, eds), New York, Cambridge University Press, 3-29.

Frenger, P. (1984), 'A short run general equilibrium model of the Norwegian production sectors', Central Bureau of Statistics, Norway.

Fullerton, D. (1979), 'A general equilibrium taxation model with applications and dynamic extensions', *Proceedings of the NTA-TIA meetings of October 1979*,249-60.

Fullerton, D. (1982), 'On the possibility of an inverse relationship between tax rates and government revenues', *Journal of Public Economics,* **19**, 3-22.

Fullerton, D. (1983), 'Transition losses of partially mobile industry-specific capital', *Quarterly Journal of Economics,* **98**, 107-25.

Fullerton, D. and Gordon, R.H. (1983), 'A re-examination of tax distortions in general equilibrium models', in *Behavioral Simulation Methods in Tax Policy Analysis,* (M. Feldstein, ed.), Chicago, University of Chicago Press.

Fullerton, D., Henderson, Y. K. and Shoven, J.B. (1984), 'A comparison of methodologies in general equilibrium models of taxation', in *Applied General Equilibrium Analysis,* (H.E. Scarf and J.B. Shoven, eds), New York, Cambridge University Press.

Fullerton, D., King, A.T., Shoven, J.B. and Whalley, J. (1981), 'Corporate integration in the United States: a general equilibrium approach', *American Economic Review* , **71**, 677-91.

Fullerton, D., Shoven, J.B. and Whalley, J. (1978), 'General equilibrium analysis of U.S. taxation policy', in *1978 Compendium of Tax research*, Office of Tax Analysis, U.S. Treasury Department, Washington, DC, U.S. Government Printing Office, 23-55.

Fullerton, D., Shoven, J.B. and Whalley, J. (1983), 'Replacing the U.S. income tax with a progressive consumption tax: a sequenced general equilibrium approach', *Journal of Public Economics,* **20**, 3-23.

Galper, H. and Toder, E. (1984), 'Transfer elements in the taxation of income from Capital', in *Economic Transfers in the United States* (Marilyn Moon, ed.), Chicago, University of Chicago Press.

Galper, H., Lucke, R. and Toder, E. (1986), 'Taxation, portfolio choice, and the allocation of capital: a general equilibrium approach', *Brookings Discussion Papers in Economics.*

Ginsburgh, V. and Waelbroeck, J. (1975), 'A general equilibrium model of world trade: Part I and II, *Cowles Foundation Discussion Paper Nos. 412 and 413,* Yale University.

Ginsburgh, V. and Waelbroeck, J. (1981), *Activity Analysis and General Equilibrium Modelling,* Amsterdam, North-Holland.

Ginsburgh, V. and Waelbroeck, J. (1984), 'Planning models and general equilibrium activity analyses', in *Applied General Equilibrium Analysis* (H.E. Scarf and J.B. Shoven, eds), New York, Cambridge University Press.

Glomsrød, S., Johnsen, R. and Vennemo, H. (1990) 'Stabilisation of emissions of CO_2: a computable general equilibrium assessment' *Discussion Paper No. 48*, Central Bureau of Statistics, Oslo (April).

Goulder, L. (1985), 'Tax-financed vs. bond-financed government spending: simulation efficiency and distributional consequences', mimeo, Harvard University.

Goulder, L. and Eichengreen, B. (1988), 'Savings promotion, investment promotion and international competitiveness', in *Trade Policies for International Competitiveness* (R. Feenstra, ed.), Chicago, Chicago University Press.

Goulder, L. and Eichengreen, B. (1989), 'Trade liberalisation in general equilibrium: intertemporal and inter-industry effects', National Bureau for Economic Research Working Paper 2695.

Goulder, L. and Summers, L. (1987), 'Tax policy , asset prices and growth: a general equilibrium analysis', National Bureau for Economic Research Working Paper no. 212.

Goulder, L.H., Shoven, J.B. and Whalley, J. (1983), 'Domestic tax policy and the foreign sector: the importance of alternative foreign sector formulations to results for general equilibrium tax analysis model', in *Behavioral Simulation Methods in Tax Policy Analysis* (M. Feldstein, ed.), Chicago, University of Chicago Press.

Grais, W., Melo, J. de and Urata, S. (1986), 'A general equilibrium estimation of the effects of reductions in tariffs and quantitative restrictions in Turkey in 1978' in *General Equilibrium Trade Policy Modelling* (T.N. Srinivasan and J. Whalley, eds), Cambridge Massachusetts: M.I.T. Press.

Greenaway, D. and Milner, C. (1993), *Trade and Industrial Policy in Developing Countries*, London, Macmillan.

Haaland, J.I., Norman, V.D., Wergeland, T. and Rutherford, T. (1988), 'VEMOD: a Ricardo-Heckscher-Ohlin-Jones model of world trade', Centre for Applied Research, Bergen.

Hamilton, R. and Whalley, J. (1985), 'Geographically discriminatory trade arrangements', *Review of Economics and Statistics*, **67**, 446-55.

Hansen, T. (1968), *On the Approximation of a Competitive Equilibrium*, unpublished PhD dissertation, Yale University

Harberger, A.C. (1959), 'The corporation income tax: an empirical appraisal', *Tax Revision Compendium 1* (House Committee on Ways and Means, 86th Congress, First Session), 231-40.

Harberger, A.C. (1962), 'The incidence of the corporation income tax', *Journal of Political Economy* , **70**, 215-40.

Harberger, A.C. (1964), 'Taxation, resource allocation and welfare', in *The Role of Direct and Indirect Taxes in the Federal Reserve System*, Princeton, Princeton University Press.

Harberger, A.C. (1966), 'Efficiency effects of taxes on income from capital', in *Effects of Corporation Income Tax* (M. Krzyzaniak, ed.), Detroit, Wayne State University Press.

Harberger, A.C. (1974), *Taxation and Welfare,* Chicago, University of Chicago Press.

Harrigan, F. (1993), 'Software for solving numerical general equilibrium models', *Economic Journal,* **103**, forthcoming.

Harris, R. (1984), 'Applied general equilibrium analysis of small open economies with scale economies and imperfect competition', *American Economic Review,* **74**, 1016-32.

Harris, R. (1985), Summary of a project on the general equilibrium evaluation of Canadian trade policy', in *Canada-United States Free Trade* (J. Whalley, ed.), Vol. 11, Macdonald Commission Volumes, Minister of Supply and Services Canada, Toronto, University of Toronto Press.

Harris, R. and Cox, D. (1984), *Trade, industrial policy and Canadian manufacturing*, Toronto, Ontario Economic Council.

Harrison, G., Rutherford, T. and Wooton, I. (1989a), 'The economic impact of the European Community', *American Economic Review*, **79**, 288-94.

Harrison, G., Rutherford, T. and Wooton, I. (1989b), 'The Common Agricultural Policy of the European Communities', Working Paper 8905C, Centre for the Study of International Economic Relations, University of Western Ontario.

Harrison, G., Rutherford, T. and Wooton, I. (1992), 'An alternative welfare decomposition for customs unions', Working Paper, University of Western Ontario.

Harrison, G.W. and Kimbell, L.J. (1983), 'How robust is numerical general equilibrium analysis?', mimeo, University of Western Ontario.

Hausman, J.A. (1983), 'Stochastic problems in the simulation of labour supply', in *Behavioral Simulation Methods in Tax Policy Analysis,* (M. Feldstein, ed.), Chicago, University of Chicago Press.

Hoeller, P. Dean, A. and Hayafuji, M. (1992), New issues, new results: the OECD's second survey of the macroeconomic costs of reducing CO_2 emissions, OECD Economics Department Working Paper no. 123.

Hoeller, P., Dean, A. and Nicolaisen, J. (1991), 'Macroeconomic implications of reducing greenhouse gas emissions: a survey of empirical studies', *OECD Economic Studies,* **16**.

Hudson, E.A. and Jorgenson, D.W (1976), 'U.S. tax policy and energy conservation', in *Econometric Studies of U.S. Energy Policy* (D.W. Jorgenson, ed.), Amsterdam, North Holland, 7-94

Hudson, E.A. and Jorgenson, D.W (1978), 'Energy prices and U.S. economy, 1972 1976', *Natural Resources Journal,* **1**, 877-897, reprinted in *U.S. Energy Policy* (W.J. Mead and E.A. Utton, eds), Cambridge, Ma., Ballinger (1979), 175-195.

Hudson, E.A. and Jorgenson, D.W. (1978), 'Energy policy and U.S. economic growth', *American Economic Review,* **68**, 118-23.

Hunter, L., Markusen, J. and Rutherford, T. (1992), 'US-Mexico Free Trade and the North American Auto Industry: Effects on the Spatial Organisation of Production of Finished Autos', *The World Economy,* **15**, 65-82.

Huntington, H.G., Weyant, J.P. and Sweeney. J.L. (1982), 'Modeling for insights, not numbers: the experiences of the energy modelling forum', *OMEGA*, *The International Journal of Management Science* , **5**, 449-62.

Intergovernmental Panel on Climate Change (IPCC) (1990), 'Policy makers summary of the scientific assessment of climate change', WMO and UNEP, New York.

IEA (1990), *Follow-up to Noordwijk Ministeral Conference on Atmospheric Pollution and Climate Change*, IEA/SLT 90/2, Paris.

James, J.A. (1978), 'The welfare effects of the ante-bellum tariff: a general equilibrium analysis', *Explorations in Economic History* , **15**, 231-56.

James, J.A. (1984), 'The use of general equilibrium analysis in economic history', *Explorations in Economic History,* **21**, 231-53.

James, J.A., and Skinner, J.S. (1984), 'The resolution of the labour scarcity paradox', *Working Paper No. 1504* Cambridge, Ma., National Bureau of Economic Research.

Johansen, L. (1960), *A Multi-Sectoral Study of Economic Growth*, Amsterdam, North-Holland.

Johansen, L. (1975), *A Multi-Sectoral Study of Economic Growth,* second edition, Amsterdam, North-Holland.

Johnson, H.G. (1954), "Optimum tariffs and retaliation', *Review of Economic Studies,* **21**, 142-153.

Johnson. H.G. (1958), *International Trade and Economic Growth: Studies in Pure Theory,* Cambridge, Harvard University Press.

Jones, R.W. (1965), 'The structure of simple general equilibrium models', *Journal of Political Economy* , **73**, 557-72

Jorgenson, D.W. (1984), 'Econometric methods for applied general equilibrium modelling', in *Applied General Equilibrium Analysis* (H.E. Scarf and J.B. Shoven, eds), New York, Cambridge University Press.

Jorgenson, D.W. and Fraumeni, B.M. (1981), 'Relative prices and technical change', in *Modelling and Measuring Natural Resource Substitution* (E. Berndt and B. Fields, eds), Cambridge, MIT Press,17-47. Reprinted in *Quantitative Studies on Production and Prices* (W. Eichhorn, R. Henn, K. Neumann, and R.W. Sheppard, eds), Wurzburg, PhysicVerlag (1983), 241-69.

Jorgenson, D.W., Lau, L.J. and Stocker, T.M. (1980), 'Welfare comparison under exact aggregation', *American Economic Review*, **70**, 268-72.

Jorgenson, D.W. and Slesnick, D.T. (1983), 'Policy alternatives for regulation and taxation of domestic petroleum production in the United States', Cambridge, Harvard Institute for Economic Research Discussion Paper No. 981.

Jorgenson, D.W. and Slesnick, D.T. (1985), 'Efficiency versus equity in economic policy evaluation', in *New Developments in Applied General Equilibrium Analysis,* (Piggot J. and Whalley, J. eds), New York, Cambridge University Press.

Jorgenson, D.W. and Wilcoxen, P.J. (1990), 'The cost of controlling US carbon dioxide emissions', Cambridge, Harvard University.

Jorgenson, D.W. and Yun, Kun-Young (1984), 'Tax policy and capital allocation', Harvard University.

Kehoe, T. (1980), 'An index theorem for general equilibrium models with production', *Econometrica* , **48**, 121 -132.

Kehoe, T. (1980), 'Index theorems and uniqueness of equilibrium', London, Ontario, University of Western Ontario, mimeo.

Kehoe, T. and Serra-Puche, J. (1983), 'A computational general equilibrium model with endogenous unemployment', *Journal of Public Economics,* **22**, 1-26.

Kehoe, T. and Whalley, J. (1982), 'Uniqueness of equilibrium in a large scale numerical general equilibrium model', London, Ontario, University of Western Ontario, mimeo.

Keller. W.J. (1980), *Tax Incidence: A General Equilibrium Approach,* North-Holland.

Kelley, A.C. and Williamson, J.G. (1983), 'A computable general equilibrium model of third world urbanization and city growth: preliminary comparative statics', in *Modelling Growing Economies in Equilibrium* and *Disequilibrium* (A. Kelley, W. Sanderson and J. Williamson, eds), Durham, NC, Duke University Press.

Kenning, S.J. and de Ruijter, W.A. (1991), 'Guidelines to the Construction of a Social Accounting Matrix', *Review of Income and Wealth,* **37**, 71-100.

Kimbell, L.J. and Harrison, G.W. (1983), 'On the solution of general equilibrium models', draft manuscript, University of Western Ontario.

Kimbell, L.J. and Harrison, G.W. (1984), 'General equilibrium analysis of regional fiscal incidence', in *Applied General Equilibrium Analysis* (H. E. Scarf and J. B. Shoven, eds), New York, Cambridge University Press.

King, A.T. (1977), 'Computing general equilibrium prices for special economies', *Review of Economics and Statistics* , **59**, 340-50.

King, A.T. (1980), 'General equilibrium with externalities: a computational method and urban application', *Journal of Urban Economics,* **7**, 84-101.

King, M. (1981), 'What is a SAM? A layman's guide to Social Accounting Matrices', *World Bank Staff Working Paper no. 463.*

King, M. and Fullerton, D (eds) (1984), *The Taxation of Income from Capital: A Comparative Study of the US, UK, Sweden and West Germany*, Chicago, Chicago University Press.

Kuhn, H.W. (1968), 'Simplicial approximation of fixed points', *Proceedings of the National Academy of Sciences, USA*, **61**, 1238-42.

Kuhn, H.W. and MacKinnon, J.G. (1975), 'The sandwich method for finding fixed points', *Journal of Optimisation Theory and Application* , **17**, 189-204

Lemke, C.E. and Howson, J.T. (1964), 'Equilibrium points of bi-matrix games', *SIAM Journal of Applied Mathematics*. **12**, 413-23.

Lewis, J. and Urata, S. (1984), 'Anatomy of a Balance of Payments Crisis: Application of a Computable General Equilibrium Model to Turkey, 1978-80', *Economic Modelling,* **1**, 281-303.

Longva, S., Lorentsen, L. and Olsen, O. (1984), 'The multi-sectoral growth model MSG-4 formal structure and empirical characteristics', Central Bureau of Statistics, Norway.

MacKinnon, J. (1974), 'Urban general equilibrium models and simplicial search algorithms', *Journal of Urban Economics,* **1**, 161 83.

Manne, A.S. (1977), 'ETA-MACRO- a model of energy economy interactions', in *Modelling Energy-Economy Interactions: Five Approaches* (Hitch, C. ed.), Washington, DC, Resources for the Future.

Manne, A.S. (1983), 'A three-region model of energy, international trade and economic growth', in *Global International Economic Models.* (B. G. Hickman, ed.), Amsterdam. North-Holland.

Manne, A.S. (1992), 'Global 2100: alternative scenarios for reducing carbon emissions', OECD Economics Department Working Papers no. 111.

Manne, A.S. and Preckel, P.V. (1983), 'A three-region intertemporal model of energy International trade and capital flows', mimeo, Department of Operations Research, Stanford University.

Manne, A.S. and Richels, R.G. (1990a), 'CO_2 emission limits: an economic cost analysis for the USA', *The Energy Journal,* **11**, 51-74.

Manne, A.S. and Richels, R.G. (1990b), 'Global CO2 emission reduction - the impacts of rising energy costs', *The Energy Journal,* **12**, 87-108.

Manne, A.S. and Richels, R.G. (1991), *Buying Greenhouse Insurance - the Economic Costs of CO_2 Emission Limits*, MIT Press.

Mansur, A. and Whalley, J. (1982), 'A decomposition algorithm for general equilibrium computation with Application to International Trade Models', *Econometrica*, **50**, 1547-57.

Mansur, A. and Whalley, J. (1984), 'Numerical specification of applied general equilibrium models: estimation, calibration and data', in *Applied General Equilibrium Analysis,* (H.E. Scarf and J.B. Shoven, eds), New York, Cambridge University Press.

McKenzie, L.W. (1959), 'On the existence of general equilibrium for a competitive market', *Econometrica* , **27**, 54-7 1 .

McLure, C.E. (1975), 'General equilibrium incidence analysis: the Harberger model after ten years', *Journal of Public Economics* , **4,** 125-62.

McLure, C.E., and Thirsk, W.R. (1975), 'A simplified exposition of the Harberger model I: tax incidence', *National Tax Journal,* **28**.

Meade, J. (1955), *The Theory of International Economic Policy,* London, Oxford University Press.

Mercenier, J. (1992), 'Completing the European internal market: a general equilibrium evaluation under alternative market structure assumption', Working paper 0892, CRDE, Université de Montréal.

Merrill, O.H. (1972), *Applications and extensions of an algorithm that computes fixed points of certain upper semi-continuous point-to-set mappings*, unpublished Ph.D. dissertation, Department of Industrial Engineering, University of Michigan.

Miller, M.H. and Spencer, J.E. (1977), 'The static economic effects of the UK joining the EEC: a general equilibrium approach', *Review of Economic Studies*, **44**, 71-93.

Mintzer, A. (1987), *A Matter of Degrees: The Potential for Controlling the Greenhouse Effect*, World Resources Institute Research Report 5, Washington DC.

Mohammad, S. and Whalley, J. (1984), 'Rent seeking in India: welfare costs and policy implications', *Kyklos*, **37**, 387-413.

Munck, S. (1982), 'The CGE-NOR model: policy issues and modelling considerations', Centre for Applied Research, Norwegian School of Economics and Business Administration, Working Paper no. 7.

Murtagh, B.A. and Saunders, M.A. (1987), 'MINOS 5.1 User's Guide', Report SOL 83-20R, Stanford University.

Nagata, Y. Yamji, K. and Sakurai, N. (1991), 'CO_2 reduction by carbon taxation and its economic impact', Economic Research Institute, Rep. No. Y91002, Central Research Institute of the Electric Power Industries.

Nguyen, T., Perroni, C. and Wigle, R.W. (1991), 'The value of a Uruguay Round success', *The World Economy*, **15**, 359-374.

Nguyen, T. and Wigle, R.W. (1989), 'Trade liberalization with imperfect competition: the large and the small of it', Research Report 89128, Wilfrid Laurier University, Waterloo, Canada.

Nordhaus, W.D. (1991a), 'To slow or not to slow: the economics of the greenhouse effect', *Economic Journal*, **101**, 920-37.

Nordhaus, W.D. (1991b), 'A survey of estimates of the costs of reduction of greenhouse gases', *The Energy Journal*, **12**, 37-65.

Oliveira Martins, J. Burniaux, J-M, Martin, J.P. and Nicoletti, G. (1992), 'The costs of reducing CO2 emissions: a comparison of carbon tax curves with GREEN', OECD Economics Department Working Paper no. 118.

Pechman, J.A. (1985), *Who pays the the taxes?*, Washington DC, Brookings Institution.

Pechman, J.A. and Okner, B.A. (1974), *Who bears the tax burden?*, Washington DC, Brookings Institution.

Peck, S. and Teisburg, T. (1991), *CETA: a model for carbon emissions trajectory assessment*, Electric Power Research Institute and Teisberg Associates.

Perroni, C. and Rutherford, T.F. (1991),'International trade in carbon emission rights and basic materials; general equilibrium calculations for 2020', mimeo, University of Western Ontario/Wilfrid Laurier University.

Persson, H. (1984), 'A version of the MSG-model with putty-clay and vintage technology', mimeo, University of Goteborg.

Piggott, J.R. (1979), 'A general equilibrium evaluation of Australian tax policy', Ph.D. dissertation, University of London.

Piggott, J.R. and Whalley, J. (1977), 'General equilibrium investigations of U.K. subsidy policy: a progress report', in *Studies in Modern Economic Analysis* (M. J. Artis and A. R. Nobay, eds), Oxford, Blackwell.

Piggott, J.R. and Whalley, J. (1985a), 'Economic effects of U.K. tax-subsidy policy: a general equilibrium appraisal', in *New Developments in Applied General Equilibrium Analysis* (J. Piggot and J. Whalley, eds), New York, Cambridge University Press.

Piggott, J.R. and Whalley, J. (1985b), *Applied general equilibrium analysis: an application. to U.K. tax policy*, New York, Cambridge University Press.

Pigott, J.R. and Whalley, J. (eds) (1985), *New Developments in Applied General Equilibrium Analysis*, New York, Cambridge University Press.

Powell, A A., Cooper, R and McLaren, K.R. (1983), 'Macroeconomic closure in applied general equilibrium modelling: experience from ORANI and agenda for further research', in *New Developments in Applied General Equilibrium Analysis* (J. Piggot and J. Whalley, eds), New York, Cambridge University Press.

Powell, A.A. (1983), 'The major streams in economy-wide modelling: is rapprochement possible?', *Large-Scale Macro Econometric Models Theory and Practice* (J. Krieta and J.B. Ramsey, eds), Amsterdam, North-Holland.

Pyatt, G. (1988), 'A SAM approach to modeling', *Journal of Policy Modeling*, **10**, 327-52.

Pyatt, G. and Round, J.I. (1977), 'Social accounting matrices for development planning', *Review of Income and Wealth,* **23**, 339-364.

Pyndick, R.S. (1973), 'Optimal policies for economic stabilisation', *Econometrica*, **41**, 529-59.

Richter, D.K. (1975), 'Existence of general equilibrium in multi-regional economies with public goods', *International Economic Review*, **16**, 201-221.

Richter, D.K. (1980), 'A computational approach to resource allocation in spacial urban models', *Regional Science and Urban Economics* , **10**, 17-42.

Robinson, S. (in press), 'Multisector Models of Developing Countries: A Survey', in H. Chenery and T.N. Srinivasan (eds), Amsterdam, North Holland.

Robinson, S. and Tyson, L. (1984), 'Modelling structural adjustment: micro and macro elements in a general equilibrium framework', in *Applied General Equilibrium Analysis* (H.E. Scarf and J.B. Shoven, eds), New York, Cambridge University Press.

Robinson, S.M. (1975), 'Newton's method for systems of nonlinear equations', in *Analysis and Computation of Equilibrium and Regions of Stability* (H. Grumm, ed.), NASA.

Rutherford, T. (1992) 'The welfare effects of fossil carbon restrictions: results from a recursively dynamic trade model', *OECD Economics Department Working Papers,* **112**.

Samuelson, P.A. (1951), 'Abstract of a theorem concerning substitutability in open Leontief models', in *Activity Analysis in Production and Allocation* (T. Koopmans, ed.), New York, John Wiley & Sons.

Scarf, H. E. and Shoven, J.B. (eds) (1984), *Applied General Equilibrium Analysis,* New York, Cambridge University Press.

Scarf, H.E. (1960), 'Some examples of global instability of the competitive equilibrium', *International Economic Review* , **1**, 157-72.

Scarf, H.E. (1967a), 'On the computation of equilibrium prices', in *Ten Economics Studies in the Tradition of Irving Fisher* (W.J. Fellner, ed.), New York, Wiley.

Scarf, H.E. (1967b), 'The approximation of fixed points of a continuous mapping', *Journal of Applied Mathematics* , **15**, 1328-43.

Scarf, H.E. (1969), 'An example of an algorithm for calculating equilibrium prices', *American Economic Review*, **59**.

Scarf, H.E. (1981), 'The computation of equilibrium prices: an exposition', in *The Handbook of Mathematical Economics,* Vol. 2 (K.J. Arrow, and M.D. Intrilligator, eds), New York, North Holland.

Scarf, H.E. (1983), 'Fixed-point theorems and economic analysis', *American Scientist*, **71**, 289-96.

Scarf, H.E. (1984), 'The computation of equilibrium prices', in *Applied General Equilibrium Analysis* (H.E. Scarf and J.B. Shoven, eds), New York, Cambridge University Press

Scarf, H.E., with the collaboration of Terje Hansen (1973), *The Computation of Economic Equilibria,* New Haven, Conn., Yale University Press.

Serra-Puche, J. (1984), 'A general equilibrium model for the Mexican economy', in *Applied General Equilibrium Analysis* (H.E. Scarf and J.B. Shoven, eds), New York, Cambridge University Press.

Shoven, J.B. (1976), 'The incidence and efficiency *effects* of taxes on income from capital', *Journal of Political Economy,* **84**, 1261-83.

Shoven, J.B. and Whalley, J. (1972), 'A general equilibrium calculation of the effects of differential taxation of income from capital in the U.S.', *Journal of Public Economics*, **9**, 281-322

Shoven, J.B. and Whalley, J. (1973), 'General equilibrium with taxes: a comput' procedure and an existence proof", *Review of Economic Studies*, **60**, 475-90.

Shoven, J.B. and Whalley, J. (1974), 'On the computation of competitive equilibrium international markets with tariffs', *Journal of International Economics,* **4**, 341-54.

Shoven, J.B. and Whalley, J. (1977), 'Equal yield tax alternatives: general equilibrium computational techniques', *Journal of Public Economics*, **8**, 211-24.

Shoven, J.B. and Whalley, J. (1984), 'Applied general equilibrium models of taxation and international trade: introduction and survey', *Journal of Economic Literature*, **52**, 1007-51.

Shoven, J.B. and Whalley, J. (1992), *Applying General Equilibrium,* Cambridge, Cambridge University Press.

Slemrod, J. (1983), 'A general equilibrium model of taxation with endogenous financial behaviour', in *Behavioral Simulation Methods in Tax Policy Analysis* (M. Feldstein, ed.), Chicago, University of Chicago Press.

Slemrod, J. (1985), 'A general equilibrium model of taxation that uses micro-unit data: with an application to the impact of instituting a flat-rate income tax', *NBER Working Paper No. 1461,* Cambridge, Ma, in *New Developments in Applied General Equilibrium Analysis* (J. Piggot and J. Whalley, eds), New York, Cambridge University Press.

Smith, A. (1990), 'The market for cars in the enlarged European Community', in *Unity with Diversity in the European Economy: The Community's Southern Frontier* (C. Bliss and G. de Masero, eds), Cambridge, Cambridge University Press.

Smith, A. and Venables, A. (1988), 'Completing the internal market in the European Community', *European Economic Review*, **32**, 1501-1525.

Smith, A. and Venables, A. (1990), 'Automobiles', in *Europe 1992: An American Perspective* (G.C. Hufbauer, ed.), Brookings Institution.

Smith, A., Venables, A. and Gasiorek, M. (1992), '1992: trade and welfare - a general equilibrium model', paper presented at the Centre for Economic Policy Research Conference on 'Trade Flows and Trade Policy', Paris.

Sobarzo, H. (1992), 'A general equilibrium analysis of the gains from trade for the Mexican economy of a North American Free Trade Area', *The World Economy,* **15**, 83-100.

Spencer, J. (1985), 'The European economic community: general equilibrium computation and the economic implications of membership', in *New Developments in Applied General Equilibrium Analysis* (J. Piggott and J. Whalley, eds), New York, Cambridge University Press.

Srinavasan, T.N. and Whalley, J. (1986), General Equilibrium Trade Policy Modeling, MIT Press.

Srinavasan, T.N., Whalley, J. and Wooton, I. (1992), 'Measuring the effects of regionalism on trade and welfare', paper presented at the GATT conference on 'Regionalism and the Global Trading System', GATT, Geneva.

Staeln, C P. (1976), 'A general equilibrium model of tariffs in a non-competitive economy', *Journal of International Economics* , **6**, 39-63.

Stiglitz, J.E. (1973), 'Taxation, corporate financial policy, and the cost of capital', *Journal of Public Economics*, **2**, 1-34.

Stuart, C. (1984), 'Welfare costs per dollar of additional tax revenue in the United States', *American Economic Review,* **74**, 352-62.

Sullivan, A. M. (1983a), 'A general equilibrium model with external scale economies in production', *Journal of Urban Economics* , **13**, 235-55.

Sullivan, A. M. (1983b), 'The general equilibrium effects of congestion externalities'. *Journal of Urban Economics* , **14**, 80-104.

Sullivan, A. M. (1983c), 'Second-best policies for congestion externalities', *Journal of Urban Economics*, **14**, 105-123.

Summers, L.H. (1982), 'Taxation and the size and composition of the capital stock: An asset price approach', mimeo, Harvard University.

Summers, L.H. (1983), 'The asset price approach to the analysis of capital income taxation', *Discussion Paper No. 1013*, Cambridge, Harvard University.

Tarr, D.G. (1989), 'A General Equilibrium Analysis of the Welfare and Employment Effects of U.S. Quotas in Textiles, Autos and Steel', *Bureau of Economics Staff Report to the Federal Trade Commission.*

Taylor, L. and Black, S.L. (1974), 'Practical general equilibrium estimation of resource pulls in trade liberalisation', *Journal of International Economics,* **4**, 37-58.

Thorbecke (1985), 'The SAM and consistency type planning models', in *Social Accounting Matrices: A Basis for Planning* (G. Pyatt and J.I. Round, eds), Washington, World Bank.

Todd, M.J. (1984), 'Efficient methods of computing economic equilibria', in *Applied General Equilibrium Analysis* (H.E. Scarf and J.B. Shoven, eds), New York, Cambridge University Press.

Treadway, A.S. (1969), 'On rational economic behaviour and the demand for investment', *Review of Economic Studies*, **36**, 227-39.

Trela, I. and Whalley, J. (1990), 'Global effects of developed country trade restrictions on textiles and apparel', *The World Economy,* **15**, 45-64.

Trela, I. and Whalley, J. (1992), 'Trade liberalisation in quota restricted items: US and Mexico in textiles and steel', *Economic Journal,* **100**, 1190-1205.

van der Lann, G. and Talman, A.J. (1979a), 'A restart algorithm for computing fixed points without an extra dimension', *Mathematical Programming* , **17**, 74-83.

van der Lann, G. and Talman, A.J. (1979b), 'A restart algorithm without an artificial lecomputing fixed points on unbounded regions', in *Functional Differential Equation Approximations of Fixed Points* (H.O. Peitgen and H.O. Walther, eds), Heidelberg-Spr. Verlag.

Vincent, D. (1982), 'A multicountry, multisector general equilibrium model system with endogenous trade', *Working Paper No.* 174, Kiel Institute of World Economics.

Venyoukas, L. (1992), 'Carbon taxes and CO2 emission targets: results fromthe IEA model', *OECD Economics Department Working Papers,* **114**.

Whalley, J. (1973), 'A numerical assessment of the April 1973 tax changes in the United Kingdom', unpublished Ph.D. dissertation, Yale University.

Whalley, J. (1975), 'A general equilibrium assessment of the 1973 United Kingdom tax reform', *Economica* , **42**, 139-61.

Whalley, J. (1977), 'A simulation experiment into the numerical properties of general equilibrium models of factor market distortions', *Review of Economics and Statistics* , **5**, 194-203.

Whalley, J. (1977), 'General equilibrium analysis of U.S.-EEC-Japanese trade and trade distorting policies: a model and some preliminary findings', Department of Economics, University of Western Ontario, Research Report 7713.

Whalley, J. (1979), 'Uniform domestic tax rates, trade distortions, and economic integration', *Journal of Public Economics,* **11**, 213-21.

Whalley, J. (1980), 'Discriminatory features of domestic factor tax systems in a goods mobile-factors immobile trade model: an empirical general equilibrium approach', *Journal of Political Economy,* **88**, 1177-1202.

Whalley, J. (1982), 'The North-South debate and the terms of trade: an applied general equilibrium approach', University of Western Ontario, Centre for the Study of International Economic Relations, *Working Paper No. 8250C.*

Whalley, J. (1985), *Trade Liberalisation Among Major World Trading Areas,* Cambridge, Ma., MIT Press .

Whalley, J. (1986), 'An evaluation of the recent Tokyo round trade agreement through a general equilibrium model of world trade involving major trading areas', *Journal of Policy Modeling.*

Whalley, J. (1987), 'Operationalising Walras: Experience with Recent Applied General Equilibrium Models', in *Advances in Econometrics* (T. Bewley, ed.), Vol. 2, Cambridge, Cambridge University Press.

Whalley, J. (1989), *The Uruguay Round and Beyond,* London, Macmillan.

Whalley, J. (1991), 'The interface between environmental and trade policies', *Economic Journal,* **101**, 180-89.

Whalley, J. (1992), 'Applied General Equilibrium Modelling in *Companion to Contemporary Economic Thought* (D. Greenaway *et al.*, eds), London, Routledge.

Whalley, J. and Wigle, R. (1991), 'The international incidence of carbon taxes', in *Global Warming: Economic Policy Responses* (R. Dornbusch and J.M. Poterba, eds.), Cambridge, Ma., MIT Press.

Whalley, J. and Wigle, R.M. (1988), 'Endogenous participation in agricultural support programs and ad valorem equivalent modelling', NBER Working Paper no. 2583, Cambridge, Ma..

Whalley, J. and Wigle, R.M. (1989), 'Cutting CO_2 emissions: the effect of alternative policy approaches', paper presented at the NBER conference on AGE modelling, San Diego.

Whalley, J. and Wigle, R.M. (1992), 'Results for the OECD comparative modelling project from the Whalley-Wigle model', OECD Economics Department Working Paper no. 121.

Whalley, J. and Yeung, B. (1984), 'External sector closing rules in applied general equilibrium models', *Journal of International Economics,* **16**, 123-38.

Wigle, R.M. (1988), 'A general equilibrium evaluation of Canada-U.S. trade liberalization in a global context', *Canadian Journal of Economics,* **21**, 539-64.

Printed in the United Kingdom for HMSO
Dd297027 11/93 C6 G3397 10170